El Greco:
100 Masterpieces

By Maria Tsaneva

First Edition

*****

I0464827

<u>**El Greco: 100 Masterpieces**</u>
*****

Foreword

El Greco is one of the not many old masters who benefit from extensive fame. Like few others, he was rediscovered from darkness by an enthusiastic faction of 19-century collectors and critics, and became one of the chosen members of the contemporary pantheon of great artists. For many later admirers, El Greco was both the archetypal Spaniard and a proto-present artist of the spirit. It was as a master who "felt the spiritual inner creation".

Native from Crete, El Greco was skilled as an icon painter. Two sure examples live to tell the tale, and these be reminiscent us of the Neo-Platonic, non-naturalistic source of his art, before he set about modeling himself into a follower of Titian and an passionate apprentice of Tintoretto, Veronese, and Jacopo Bassano. He moved to Venice in 1567 (Crete was a Venetian territory). There he set about mastering the elements of Renaissance painting, including perspective, figural construction, and the ability to stage elaborate narratives. Among his finest works of this period is The Miracle of Christ Healing the Blind. Later, in Spain, El Greco wrote treatises on painting. Although these are lost, we possess the copies he owned of the architectural treatise by the ancient writer Vitruvius and Vasari's Lives. They have El Greco's annotations in the margins.

From Venice, El Greco moved to Rome, where he worked from 1570 to 1576. He arrived with a letter of recommendation from the Croatian miniaturist Giulio Clovio, who secured him quarters in the palace of Cardinal Alessandro Farnese — perhaps the most influential and wealthy patron in all of Rome. In 1572, he joined the painter's academy and he set up shop, taking on at least one assistant, and possibly two. His intention must have been to pursue a Roman career, but after six years he had not received a single commission for an altarpiece; his reputation was based on occasional commissions for portraits and small-scale devotional paintings. El Greco had ill-advisedly criticized Michelangelo's abilities as a painter, an opinion that generated little confidence in his abilities and may have served to ostracize him from the Roman art
Establishment (Michelangelo had died in 1564, but his prestige in Rome was undiminished).

These were not auspicious beginnings for his career in Spain, where he moved in 1576. In Madrid, his bid for royal patronage from Philip II failed. Not until he settled in Toledo did El Greco meet with the success an artist of his caliber might have expected. In this ancient city, which El Greco immortalized in one of the most celebrated landscapes in Western art—the View of Toledo - he found a sympathetic circle of intellectual friends and patrons and forged a highly profitable career. Diego de Castilla, dean of Toledo Cathedral, commissioned El Greco to paint three altarpieces for the Church of Santo Domingo el Antiguo in Toledo and was also instrumental in the commission of the Espolio (The Disrobing of Christ) for the cathedral bestiary. These are among El Greco's most ambitious masterpieces. In them can be found all of the various styles with which he had experimented in Italy: the naturalism that characterized his portraits; the painterly technique he had learned in Venice; the audacious compositional ideas of the late Michelangelo; and a Mannerist emphasis on extremely elegance and refinement. A dispute over the price El Greco demanded for the Espolio led to litigation and left a mark on the artist's subsequent career: he never received another comparable commission from the cathedral authorities; in the future, his commissions were to come from private individuals and convents in the city.

El Greco's most celebrated painting, The Burial of Count Orgaz, was commissioned by the parish priest of Santo Tom? in Toledo in 1586 to celebrate the restitution of a financial obligation to the church. It honors a long-dead benefactor, at whose funeral Saints Stephen and Augustine were seen to miraculously appear to assist in the burial. The picture depicts this miracle as well as the count's soul being received into Paradise. When seen in the church, the painting has the impressive character of a vision. El Greco's son Jorge kneels fictively on the edge of the picture plane, looking out and indicating to the viewer the miracle El Greco has conjured up. The figure thus serves as intermediary between the real world of the viewer and the fictional world of the painting, which gains added resonance through the inclusion of a series of portraits of El Greco's contemporaries. Above the funeral is depicted a heavenly vision, where a very different visionary experience is depicted: the verisimilitude of the earthly event is rejected in favor of a world of shifting planes inhabited by chimera-like personages. The Burial of Count Orgaz is central to our understanding of El Greco because it encapsulates the object of his art, which is to suggest a visionary experience — something that is not an extension of our physical world but of our imaginative faculties.

Toledo was far removed from the artistic ferment of Rome, but it was no bastion against the forces — cultural as well as artistic — that was to shape the art of the seventeenth century. It is all too easy to treat El Greco's achievement in isolation, as though it were an art outside of its time — an art waiting to be discovered by the modern era. Yet when El Greco died in 1614, Caravaggio and Annibale Carracci — the creators of the new Baroque style — had been buried for four and five years, respectively. It is enough to mention these figures to realize that in important respects El Greco's art belonged to the past, not the future: to the world of Mannerism, with its emphasis on the artist's imagination rather than the reproduction of nature. Francisco Pacheco — painter, artist's biographer, and teacher of Velazquez — visited El Greco in his studio in Toledo and recorded seeing plaster, wax, and clay figures from which he worked. Pacheco did not approve of this method, which El Greco had doubtless learned from Tintoretto in Venice: a real human figure rather than something modeled in clay was what Pacheco advocated. But he could not deny El Greco's place among the great painters, "for we see some works by his hand so plastic and so alive (in his characteristic style) that they equal the art of the very best." He may have had in mind El Greco's portraits, which Velazquez prized highly. Yet it is the most extravagant late works of the artist, such as The Opening of the Fifth Seal in which the figures are elongated beyond credibility and their forms dematerialized by a flickering brushwork, that have appealed so strongly to modern tastes.

El Greco discarded naturalism as a medium for his art just as he unwanted the idea of an art effortlessly easy to get to to a huge crowd. What Greco valued was the world of a self-intentionally, intellectual style, or so called maniera. The irony is that, at a time when the obvious show of inherent in Mannerism was being claimed as an extravagance, and artists in Rome were motivated to rid their works of anything that might seem plain display, El Greco took just the contradictory course. He complete extended, smoothly curved forms placed in dramatic angle and dreamlike colors are the fundament of his art. The distinction was that Greco made these things genuinely expressive and not simply emblems of his virtuosity.

There no other great Western painter who transformed spiritually — as El Greco did — from the plane figurative art of Orthodox icons to the vivid and human loving visualization of Renaissance art. His originality is founded on his denial of the world of simple appearance in favor of the kingdom of the intellectuality and the sublime humanistic ideals.

Paintings

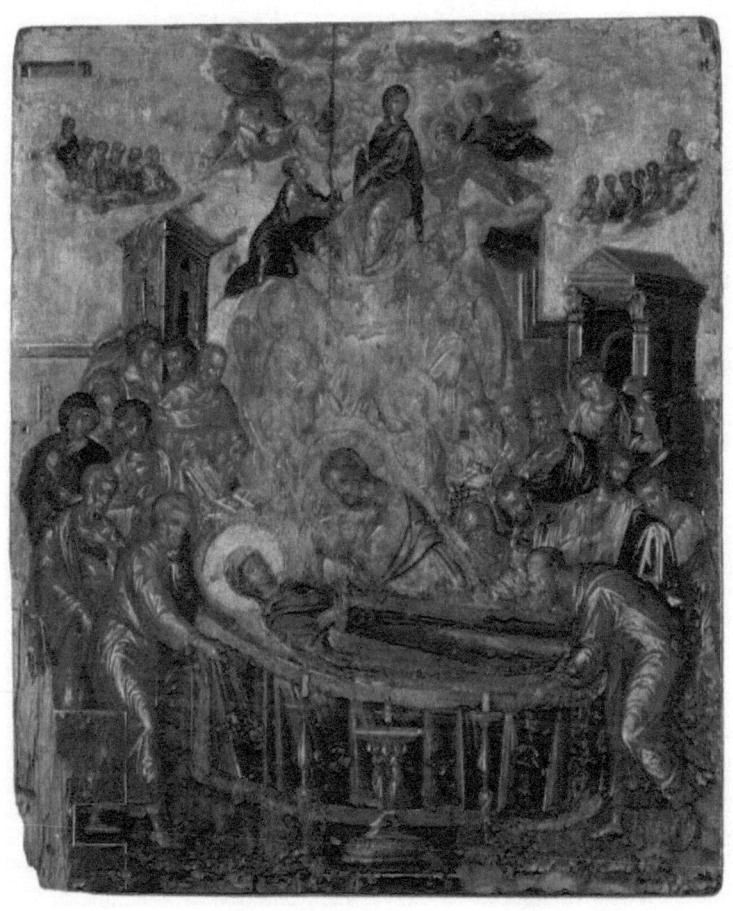

The Dormition of the Virgin, before 1567, Tempera and
gold on panel, 61, 4 x 45 cm

El Greco' signature on the base of the central candelabrum was discovered in 1983. This discovery constituted a significance advance in the understanding of El Greco's early career and formation. In both its iconography and technique the painting demonstrates the artist's origins and training in the traditions of post-Byzantine painting. The icon, which retains its function as an object of veneration in the Church of the Dormition of the Virgin on the island of Syros in the Aegean Sea south-east of Athens, was probably brought to Syros during the Greek Revolution in 1824 from the Monastery of the Holy Mountain of the Dormition of the Virgin on the island of Psara in the Aegean. The icon conforms closely to the established pattern for this subject, which was very common in the Orthodox Church in which El Greco was raised.

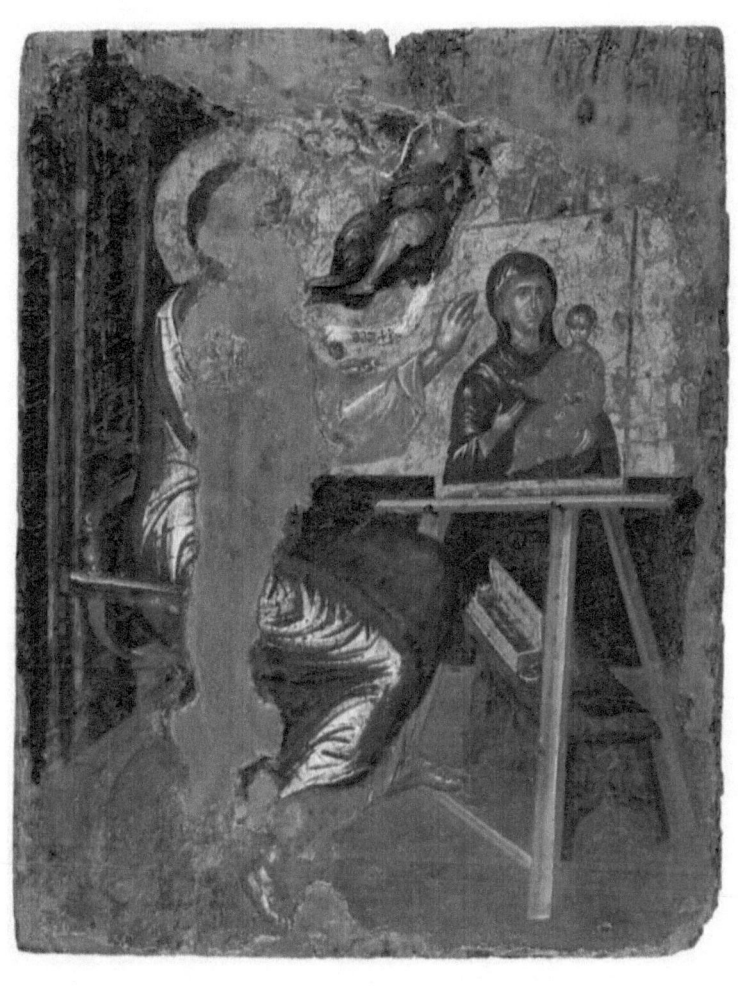

St Luke Painting the Virgin and Child, before 1567,
Tempera and gold on canvas attached to panel, 41, 6 x
33 cm

Together with the icon of The Dormition at Syros, this is one of El Greco's earliest works, painted while he was a master in Crete. It suffered serious losses but much of the paint surface remains intact and legible. It is signed in the area of the stool under the easel. It shows St Luke, traditionally both a physician and a painter, in the act of painting the icon of The Virgin Hodigitria, patron and protector of Constantinople. El Greco kept strictly to the Byzantine canon in the representation of the icon on the easel, but he allowed himself greater freedom in the rest of the depiction. This icon is a transitional work that demonstrates how the artist was seeking to graft Renaissance elements (taken from Italian prints) on to Byzantine compositions.

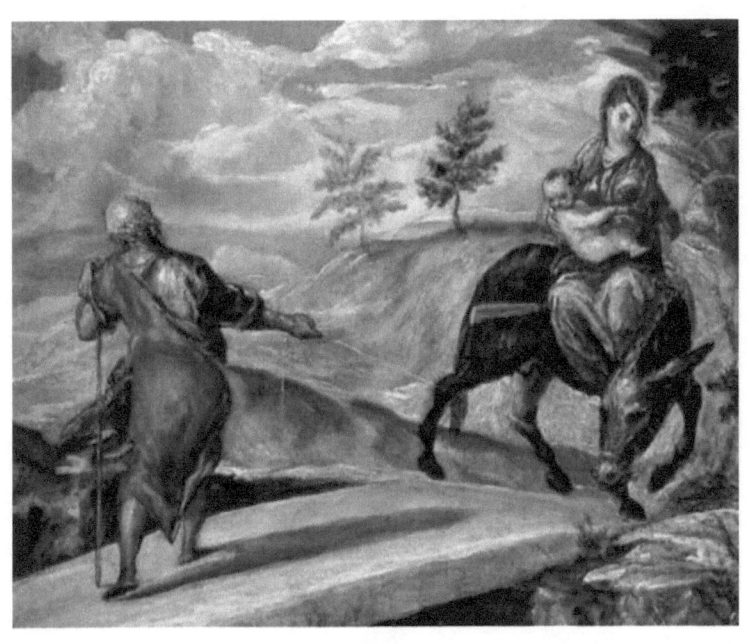

Flight into Egypt, 1567, oil on canvas

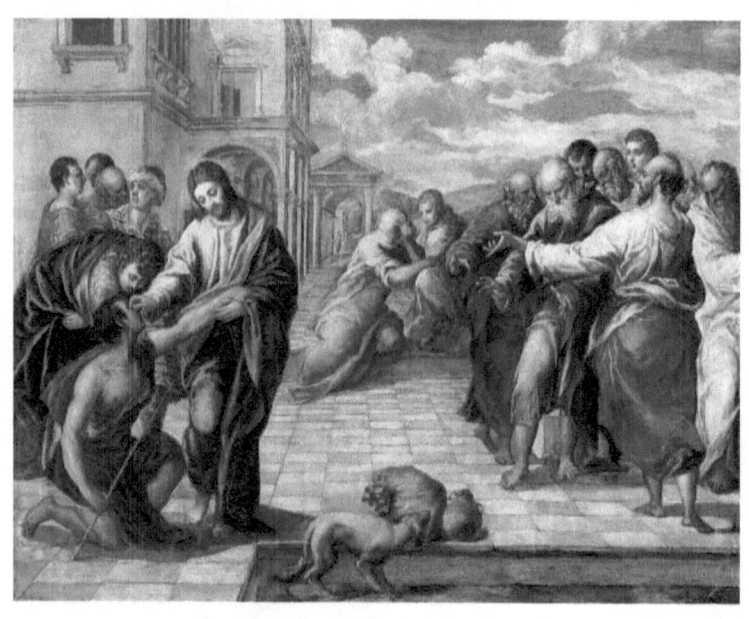

Christ Healing the Blind, c. 1567, Oil on panel

Three versions of this subject are known, all basically
the same in composition, but differing in treatment.
The earliest, an unsigned panel in Dresden, is looser in
composition, smaller in conception, and introduces
genre motifs of a dog, sack and pitcher in the
foreground, eliminated in subsequent versions. This
painting was executed under the influence of Venetian
painting, in the 17th century it was attributed to Paolo
Veronese, later to Jacopo Bassano.

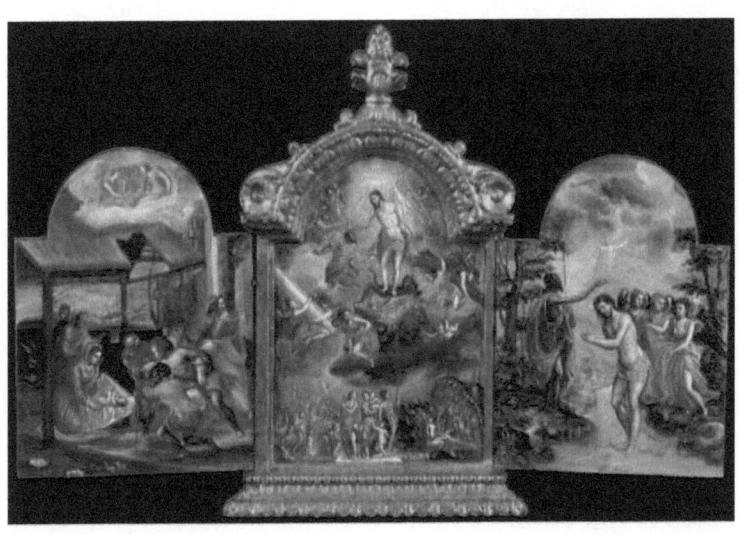

The Modena Triptych (front panels), 1568, Tempera on panel

Small portable altarpiece with hinged wings, painted on both sides, of a type similar in form to others produced in Crete in the sixteenth century, but with an Italian Renaissance frame. The subjects on the front, from left to right, are the Adoration of the Shepherds, the Allegory of a Christian Knight, and the Baptism; and on the back, the Annunciation, Mount Sinai, and Adam and Eve.

The central panel on the front, showing the Christian Knight received into Heaven, with Purgatory and Inferno below, and the three Theological virtues, is of medieval inspiration, and precisely follows a known representation of the subject. The Jaws of Hell are a specifically medieval motif. Saint Catherine, with the Wheel of her Martyrdom, appears below the figures of Christ and the Knight. The theme of Mount Sinai, on the back of the central panel, was of Cretan origin, and faithfully repeats a traditional Byzantine model. The reference to Saint Catherine in both the central panels has been suggested as a possible indication of the artist's connection in Crete with the monastery of Saint Catherine, a dependency of that of Mount Sinai, and the most important school of painting in the island. The other compositions are similarly not original, but here the artist has used engravings after Italian (mainly Venetian) compositions as his models. The repetition of traditional images was usual in Byzantine art.

The Triptych is interesting as one of the earliest known work by El Greco. It clearly belongs to the time soon after his arrival in Italy. We see the artist acquainting himself with the new Italian subject matter and its treatment, and making his first essays in the new technique of Venice. The flat, linear, geometrical designs of Byzantine art give way to compositions employing rounder, more solid forms, and a looser handling. The somewhat nervous quality may be regarded as El Greco's own, and the Triptych does contain motifs and compositions that he later develops. The subjects of the Annunciation, Adoration of the Shepherds and Baptism inspire some of El Greco's grandest works. The Allegory of the Christian Knight is appropriately recollected in the Allegory of the Holy League. The Byzantine image of Mount Sinai is not unreasonably brought to mind in front of the late Toledo.

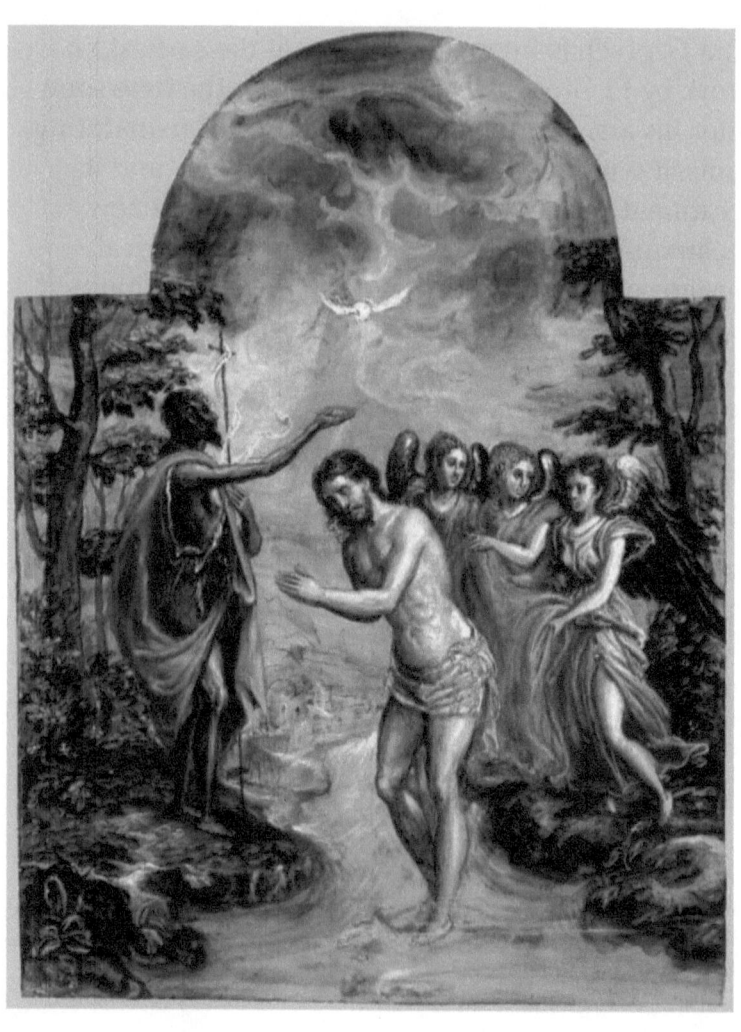

Baptism of Christ, 1568, Tempera on panel,

The Baptism of Christ is the right panel on the front of the Modena Triptych. The Modena Triptych strikingly illustrates El Greco's transition from post-Byzantine icon painter to European artist of the Latin variety. The portable altarpiece, whose unknown patron perhaps stemmed from a Creto-Venetian family, in its open state shows a total of six scenes: on the front, the central panel bears a rare depiction of the Coronation of the Christian Knight, and on the wings we find the Adoration of the Shepherds on the left and the Baptism of Christ on the right. On the reverse, a View of Mount Sinai with its famous convent of St Catherine is flanked by an Annunciation and an Admonition of Adam and Eve by God the Father. This type of object with its gilded frame elements was common in Cretan workshops of the 16th century, as is its use of wood as a painting support.

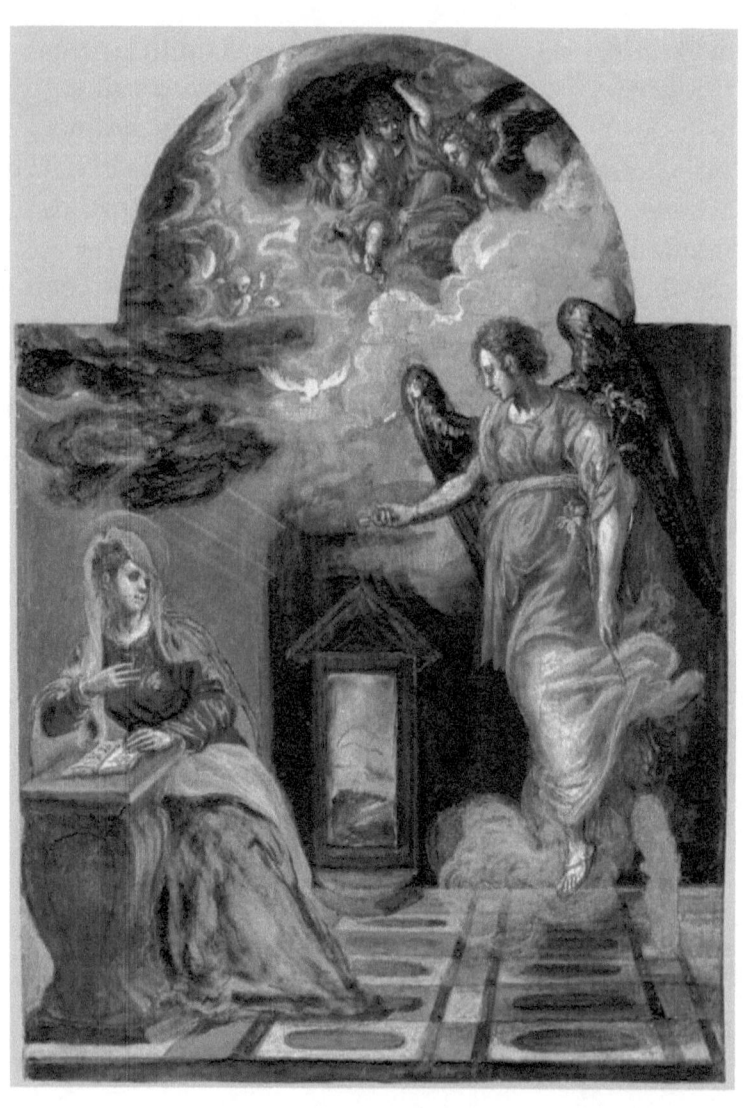

Annunciation, 1568, Tempera on panel,

Probably El Greco painted soon after his arrival in Venice the Modena Triptych. Here he adapts Renaissance principles of representation to a small-scale triptych of a post-Byzantine design common in the Venetian empire. As the wings of the triptych are opened in succession, the sequence of images reveals the state of Man before the fall to his restoration to a state of Grace through Christ. The scene of The Annunciation is the left panel on the back of the triptych.

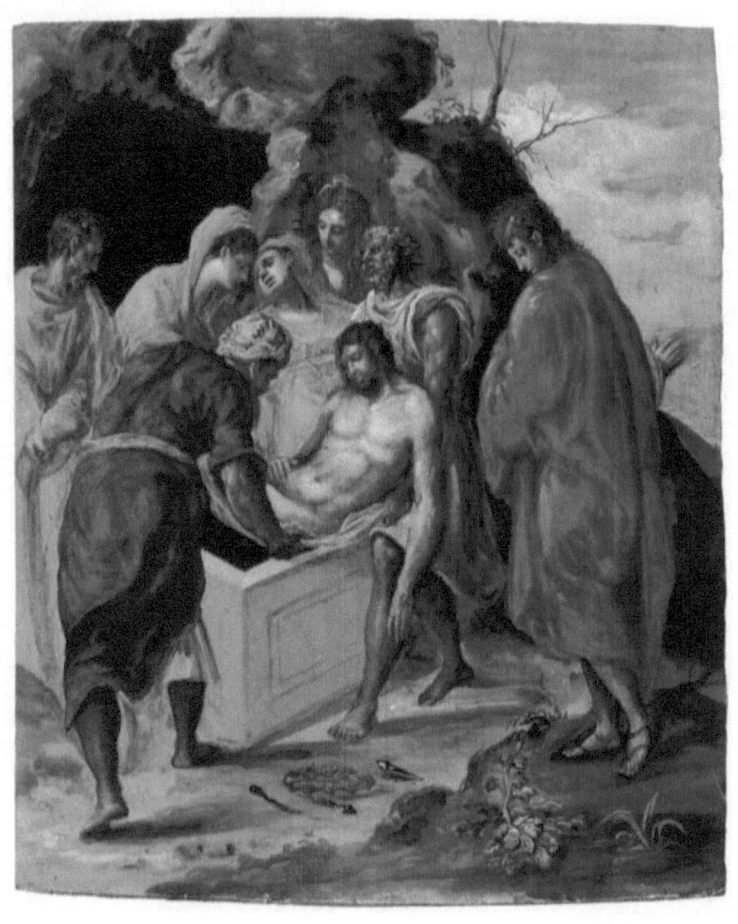

The Entombment of Christ, late 1560s, Oil and tempera on panel, 51, 5 x 43 cm

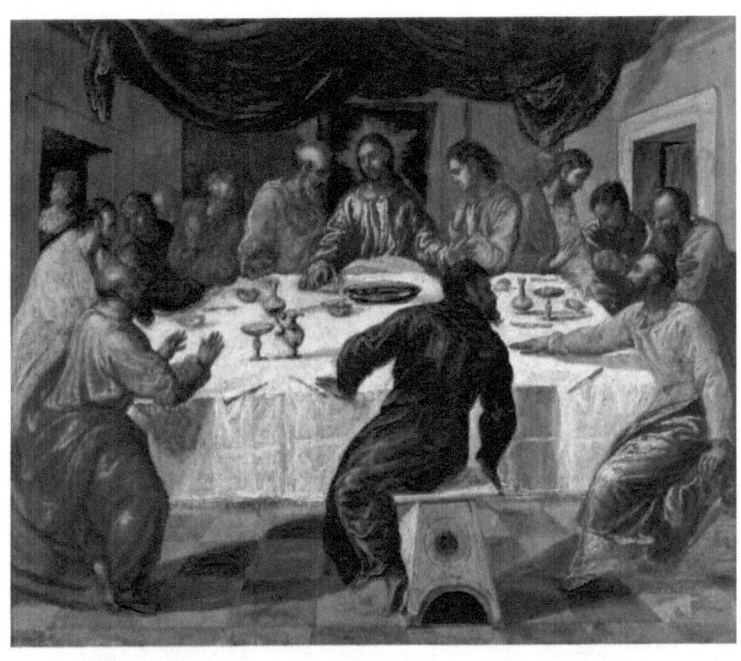

The Last Supper, c. 1568, Oil on panel

This unsigned painting evinces a similar technique as the signed ("by the hand of Domenikos") Modena Triptych, which is a key reference work for the early paintings of El Greco. In the Last Supper the perspective space is still quite simply structured. The figures have little corporeal volume and seem more to hover than actually to sit at the long table.

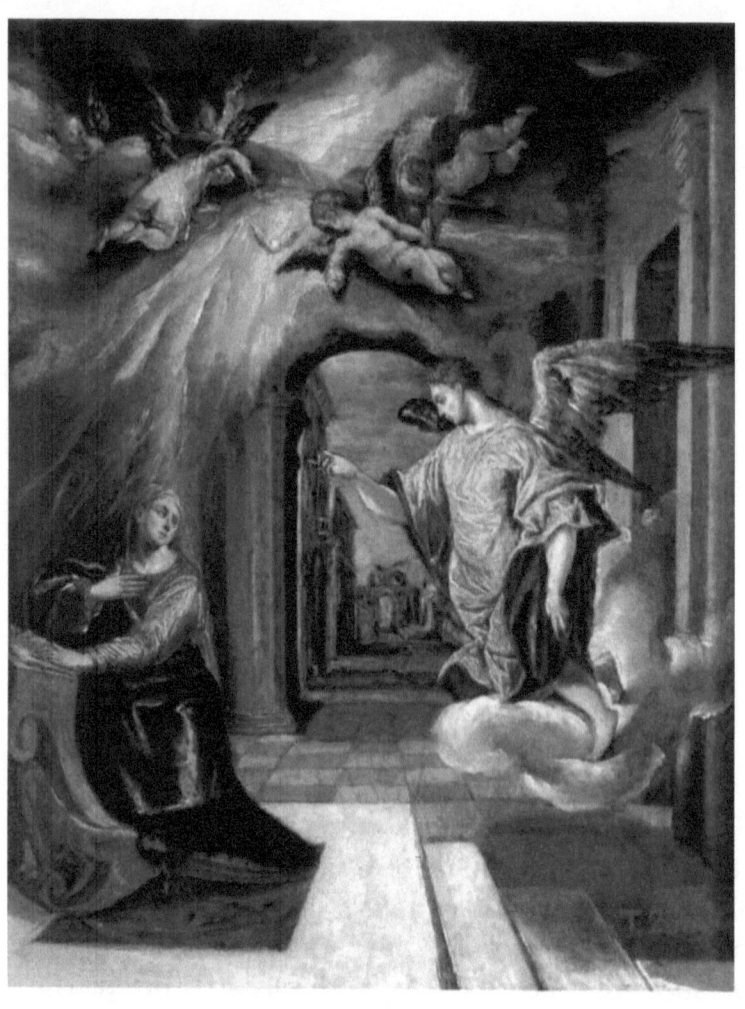

The Annunciation, c. 1570, Tempera on panel

This very small panel is probably the most completely Venetian of his paintings, and, almost certainly, was finished shortly before leaving for Rome at the end of 1570. With its comparatively robust figures and the perspective of its pavement sharply receding into the background, it provides a good contrast with his later Spanish works. The Annunciation was one of the themes most in harmony with his genius, inspiring some of his most splendid paintings.

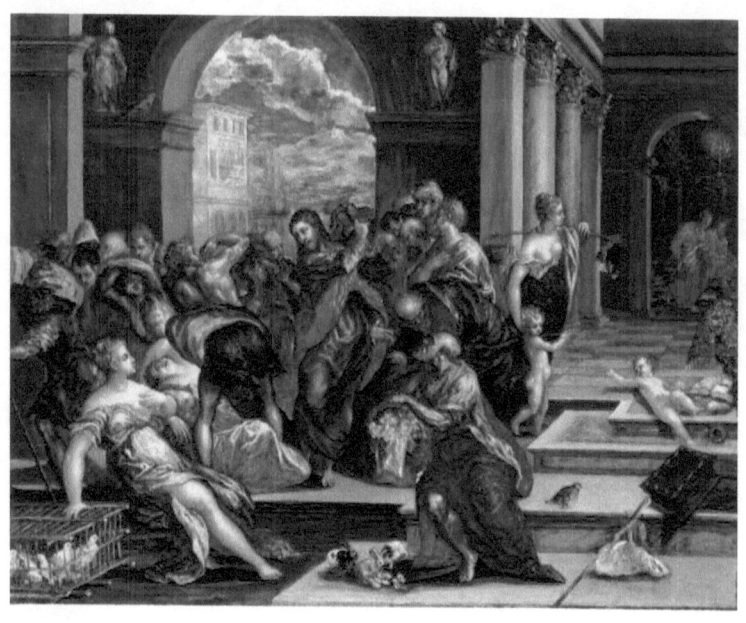

The Purification of the Temple, c. 1570, Oil on poplar
panel, 65 x 83 cm

El Greco painted several pictures of The Purification of
the Temple. The subject, which evidently held a deep
fascination for El Greco, accompanied the artist
throughout his career: he painted some versions in Italy
(possibly even in Venice) and several more dating from
the 1590s onwards - in Spain. Many more was painted
in his studio. The catalogue raisonnй of El Greco's
works lists four as autograph and eight as studio
pictures or copies.

This is the earliest known version of this subject by El Greco. It has usually been dated to El Greco's Venetian years, although some scholars have placed it to his time in Rome. The artist borrowed extensively from High Renaissance visual models (among others from Michelangelo, Titian, Veronese and Tintoretto) and did very little to disguise them. Uncertainties in the handling of anatomy and space can be observed which confirm the early date of the painting.

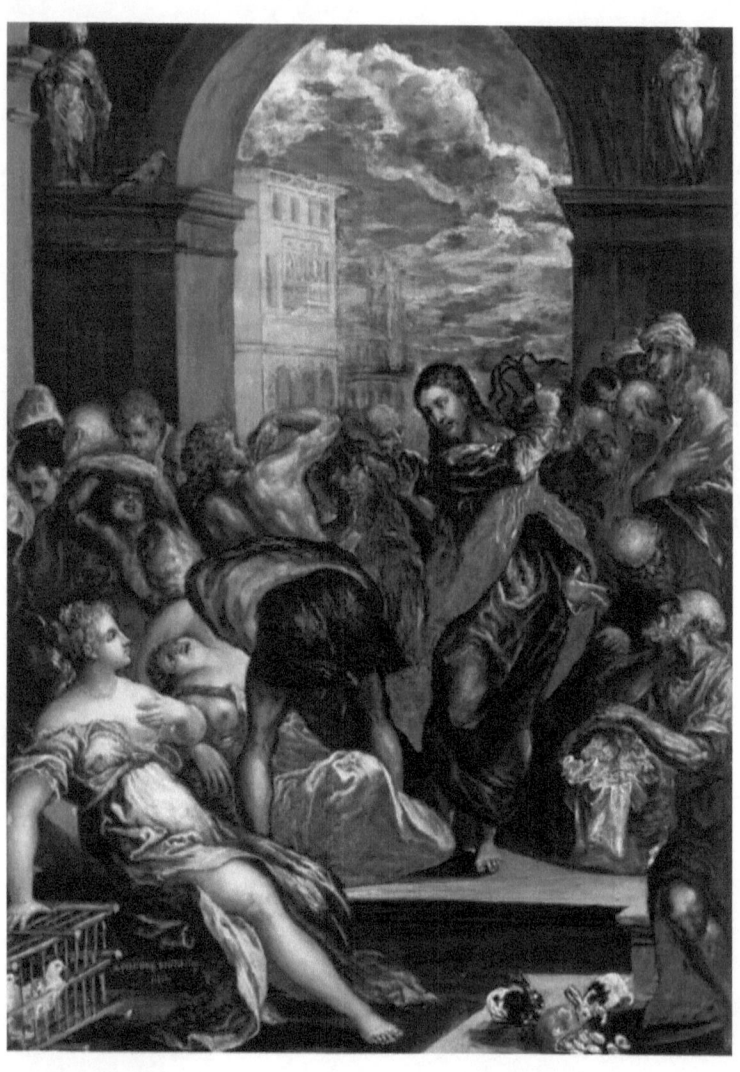

The Purification of the Temple (detail), c. 1570, Oil on poplar panel

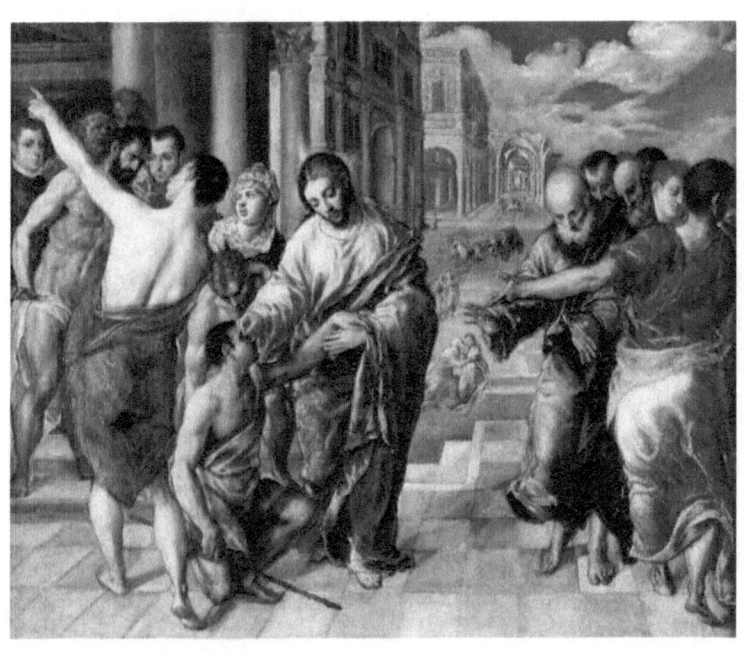

Christ Healing the Blind, 1570-75, Oil on canvas, 50 x 61
cm

Possibly the sequel to the Christ driving the Traders
from the Temple (Matthew, XXI, 14: 'And the blind and
the lame came to him in the temple; and he healed
them'). Both subjects were treated by El Greco more
than once in Italy. This is the smallest known painting
on canvas by El Greco. The painting has been cut and
the group on the right is incomplete. No large-scale
works are known from his Italian period, and most are
quite small. He does not appear to have received any
important commissions before he moved to Spain.

Three versions of this subject are known, all basically the same in composition, but differing in treatment. The earliest, an unsigned panel in Dresden, is looser in composition, smaller in conception, and introduces genre motifs of a dog, sack and pitcher in the foreground, eliminated in subsequent versions. The present painting, probably also painted in Venice, is more easily composed. The third and largest painting, now in the Metropolitan Museum in New York (possibly identical with the one in a Madrid collection at the time of Cossio's pioneer work on El Greco), with its comparative largeness of conception, belongs to his Roman period, after 1570. El Greco did not again take up the subject in Spain.

The inspiration is from Venice. The dramatic use of recession behind the figures in the foreground is Tintoretto's invention. El Greco is still borrowing certain motifs, but the composition would seem to be original. The painting was among the Farnese possessions in the seventeenth century, and was probably brought to Rome by the artist, unless it was painted soon after his arrival in 1570. The figure on the extreme left, looking out towards the spectator, is certainly the young El Greco. He appears, however, nearer twenty than thirty years old.

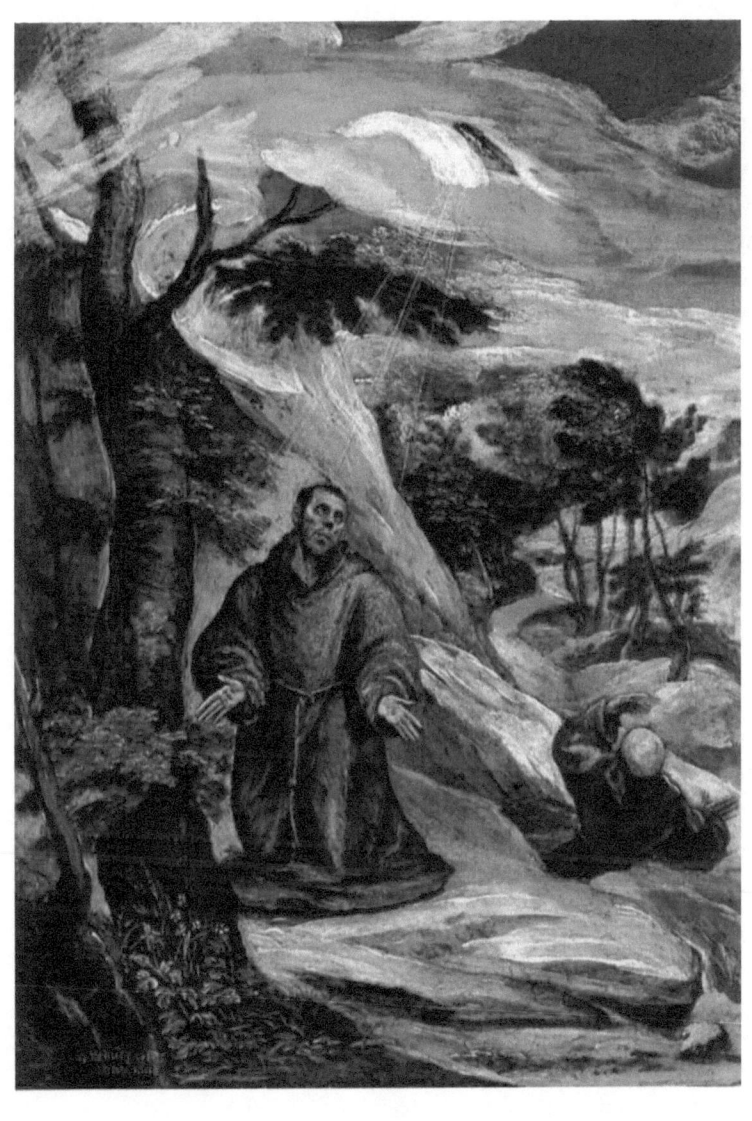

St Francis Receiving the Stigmata, 1570-72, Tempera on panel, 28,8 x 20,6 cm

Like his other devotional paintings executed on panel, El Greco almost certainly painted this picture as an image for private and intimate contemplation. Its technique is similar to that of icon painting, displaying a highly finished, enamel-like surface. The painting, signed on the lower left, was probably executed in the early 1570s soon after his arrival in Rome.

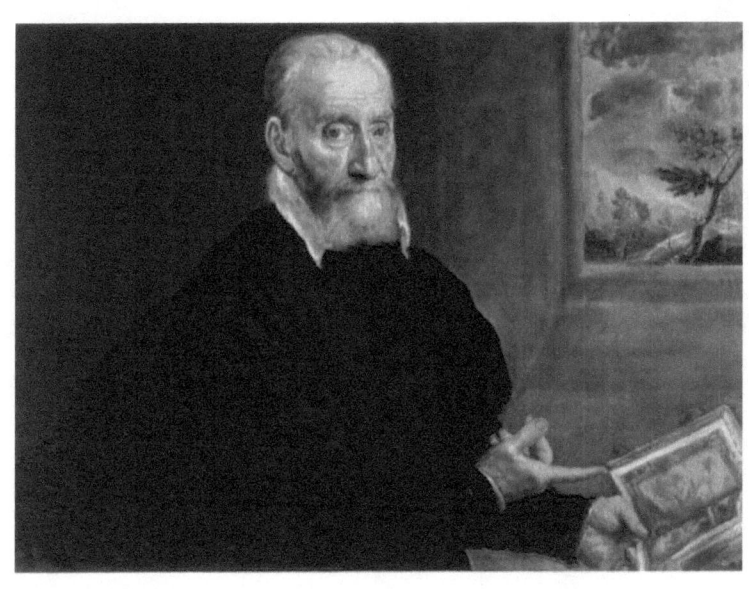

Giulio Clovio
1571-72, Oil on canvas, 58 x 86 cm
Giulio Clovio (1498-1578), a 'Greek' from Croatia, friend
of El Greco's, worked as a miniaturist in the Farnese
Library. He is portrayed holding an open book, his
most famous work, an illuminated manuscript the
Libro della Vergine, known as the Farnese Hours (at
the time in the Farnese Library, and now in the The
Morgan Library and Museum, New York). The book is
shown open at folios 59v, showing God the Father
creating the Sun and Moon, and 60r, showing the Holy
Family.

The portrait was painted probably soon after El Greco arrived in Rome (November 1570), and almost certainly for his friend. In the seventeenth century, it was in the possession of Fulvio Orsini, librarian to Cardinal Farnese. This is perhaps the earliest independent portrait by the artist who was to become one of the greatest portrait painters of all time. Three splendid portraits belong to his Italian years: the present portrait, possibly the earliest, and the signed portrait of a man in Copenhagen, both Titianesque; and the more personal Vincentio Anastagi, a signed portrait in the Frick Collection, New York. It is unfortunate that the self-portrait mentioned by Giulio Clovio is lost.

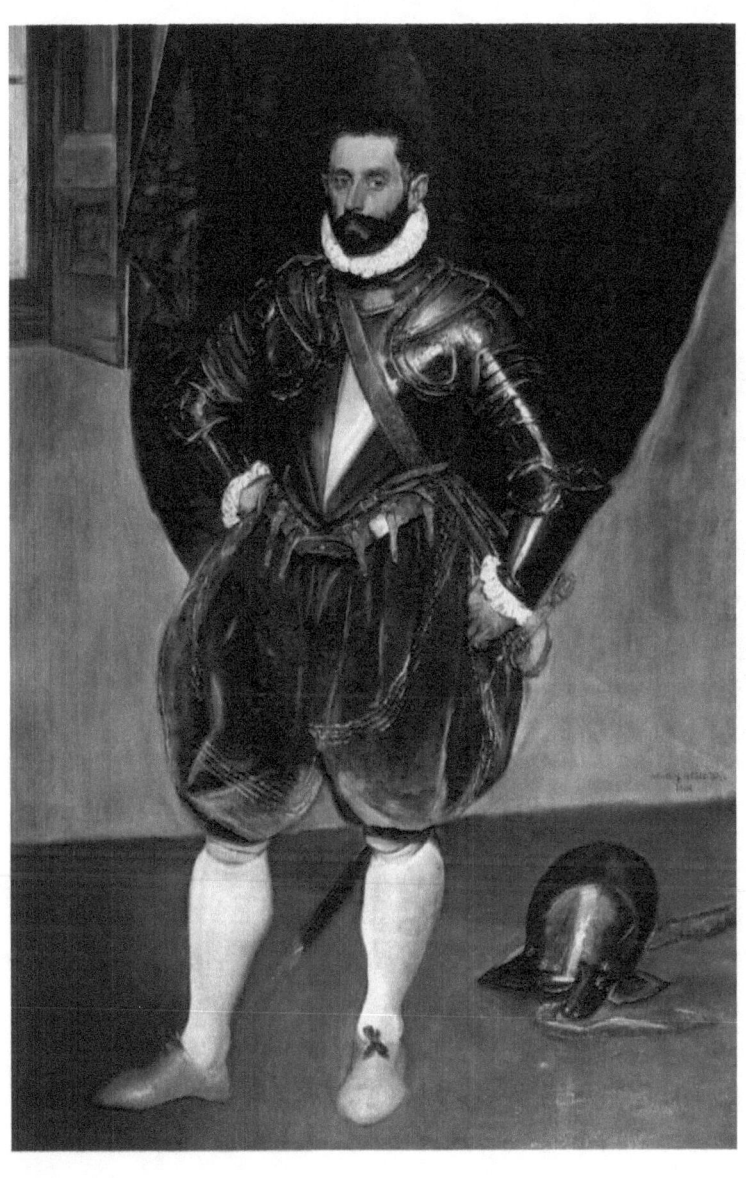

Vincenzo Anastagi, 1571-76, Oil on canvas, 188 x 127 cm

El Greco arrived in Rome in 1570 and he was recommended by Giulio Clovio to his patron Cardinal Alessandro Farnese as a portrait painter. His portraiture developed dramatically during his Roman sojourn, reaching a peak in his portrait of Vincenzo Anastagi. The sitter was a distinguished Knight of Malta, who had been appointed 'sergente maggiore' of Castel Sant'Angelo in 1575. The portrait was probably painted to commemorate the appointment. For El Greco it was an important challenge, for he seems never previously to have painted a full-length or military or official portrait.

The armour, sword, helmet, the green baldric and velvet breeches ornamented with gold thread, are the attributes of his station. Yet El Greco has not confined himself to replicating these particulars. He has sought to make manifest Anastagi's body politic as well - in particular the cardinal virtue of fortitude, comprising courage, endurance and physical strength.

In spite of the qualities of the portrait, the paucity of the extant and recorded portraits which El Greco painted in Rome suggests that commissions were not forthcoming, probably because his Titianesque technique was not appreciated.

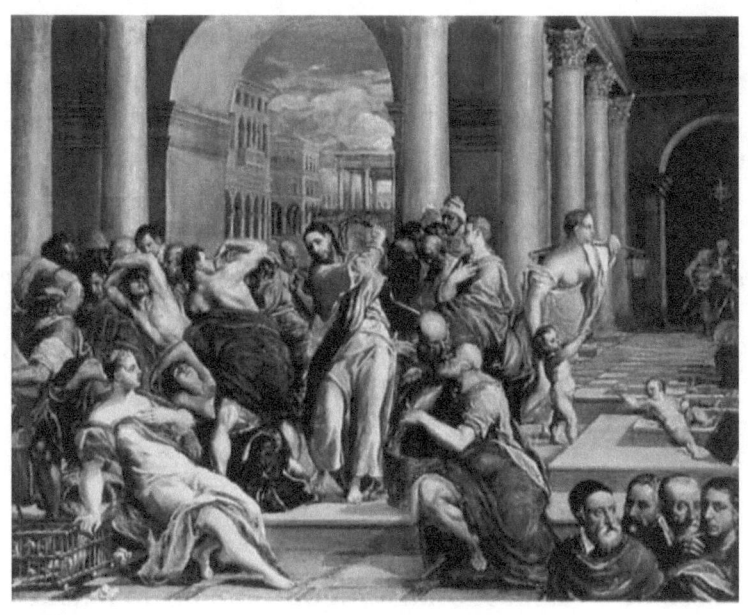

Christ drives away merchants from the Temple, 1571-
76, oil on canvas

El Greco first painted the subject in Venice, some years earlier, in the small signed panel in Washington, and he was to take it up again, much later, in Spain, and adhere closely to his original design. As with the Christ Healing the Blind, inspiration for the composition as a whole is from Tintoretto. The main central group, however, is very close to a Michelangelo design, known in drawings, and also in Venusti's painting after Michelangelo's design (National Gallery, London). The figure of the woman walking with a child could be a reminiscence of a similar motif in Raphael's tapestry cartoon, the Distributing of Alms at the Golden Gate. The two men in conversation, who also appear in the middle distance of Christ healing the Blind, have become a grand subsidiary motif, and again hint at acquaintance with Raphael. The larger forms of the architecture also derive from Raphael and Rome, and are consonant with the grander conception of the one integrated action of the main group of figures.

The four portraits at the bottom right represent, from left to right, Titian, Michelangelo, Giulio Clovio and possibly El Greco himself. The introduction of Titian and Michelangelo is clearly an acknowledgment of his debt to these two artists. To his friend, Giulio Clovio, he owed his introduction to the Farnese household. The young man looking out, pointing to himself has similar features to the self-portrait in the Christ healing the Blind at Parma, but the long hair is strange. It has also been suggested that he could represent the young Raphael. The portraits of Titian and Michelangelo (died 1564) were taken from existing portraits, and that of Giulio Clovio follows closely El Greco's portrait of his friend in the Naples Museum, painted c. 1571. El Greco does continue to include portraits in his paintings of religious subjects, but here there is no proper connection with the subject matter.

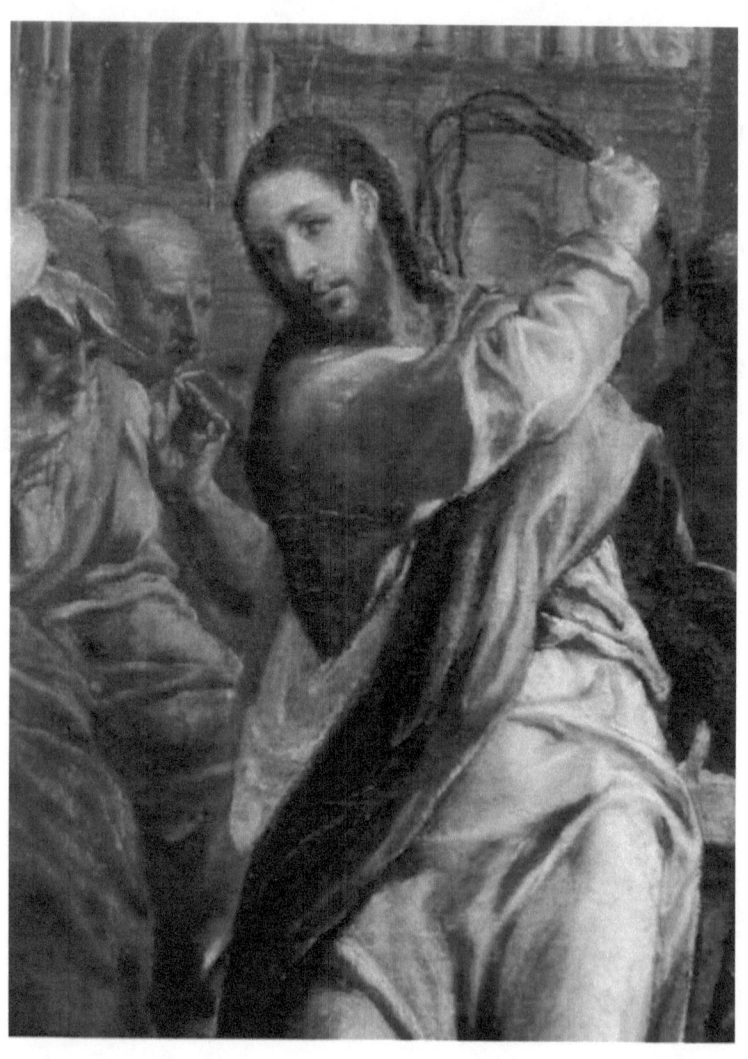

Christ drives away merchants from the Temple
(fragment), 1570, oil on canvas

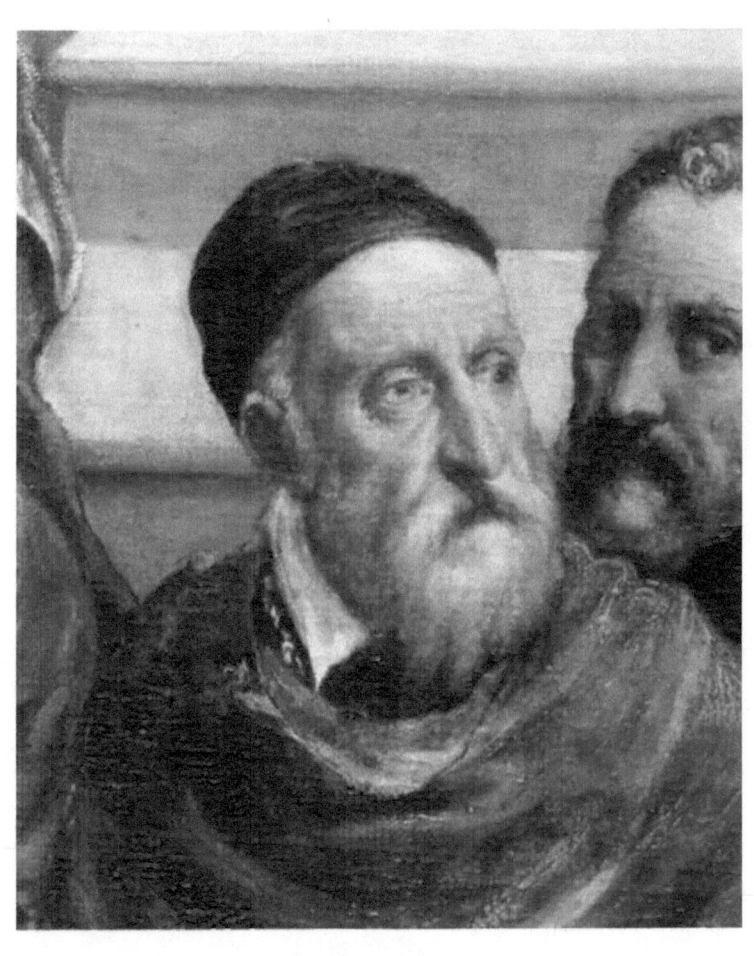

Christ drives away merchants from the Temple
(fragment), 1570, oil on canvas

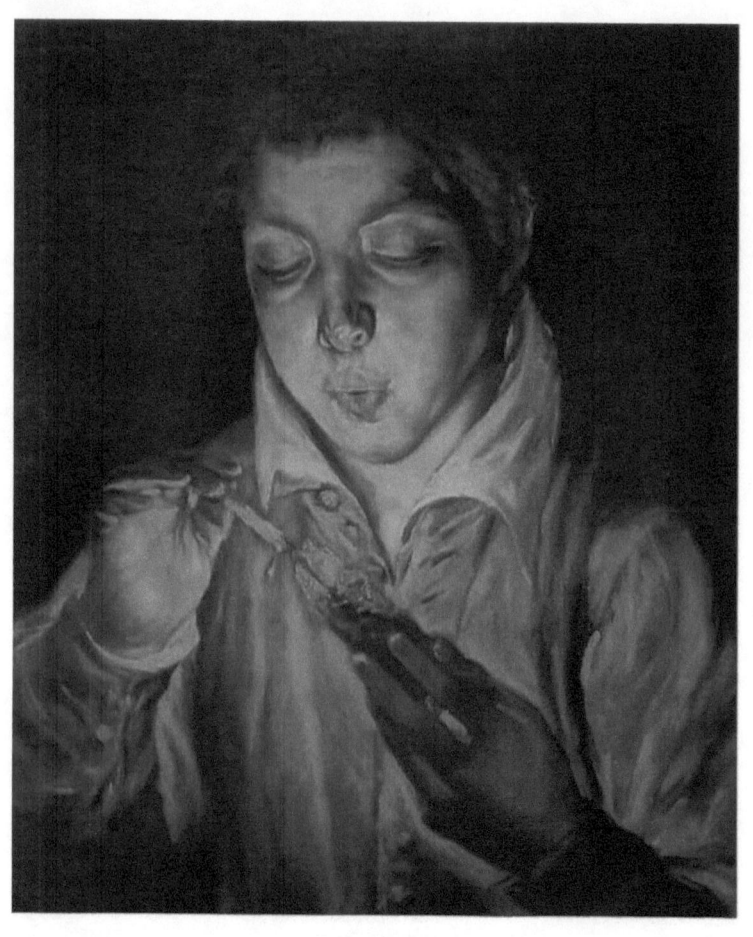

A Boy Blowing on an Ember to Light a Candle, 1572, oil on canvas

The instigator of this painting, representing a boy pursing his fleshy lips to blow on the ember in order to light the black wick of a candle, of which the wax is already melting on account of the heat, may have been Fulvio Orsini, the librarian of Cardinal Alessandro Farnese in whose palace El Greco resided between 1570 and 1572. The title 'Soplyn' (Blower) was given in Jorge Manuel's inventory. The subject of a boy blowing on an ember appears frequently as a subsidiary element in subject pictures in mid-sixteenth-century Venetian painting.

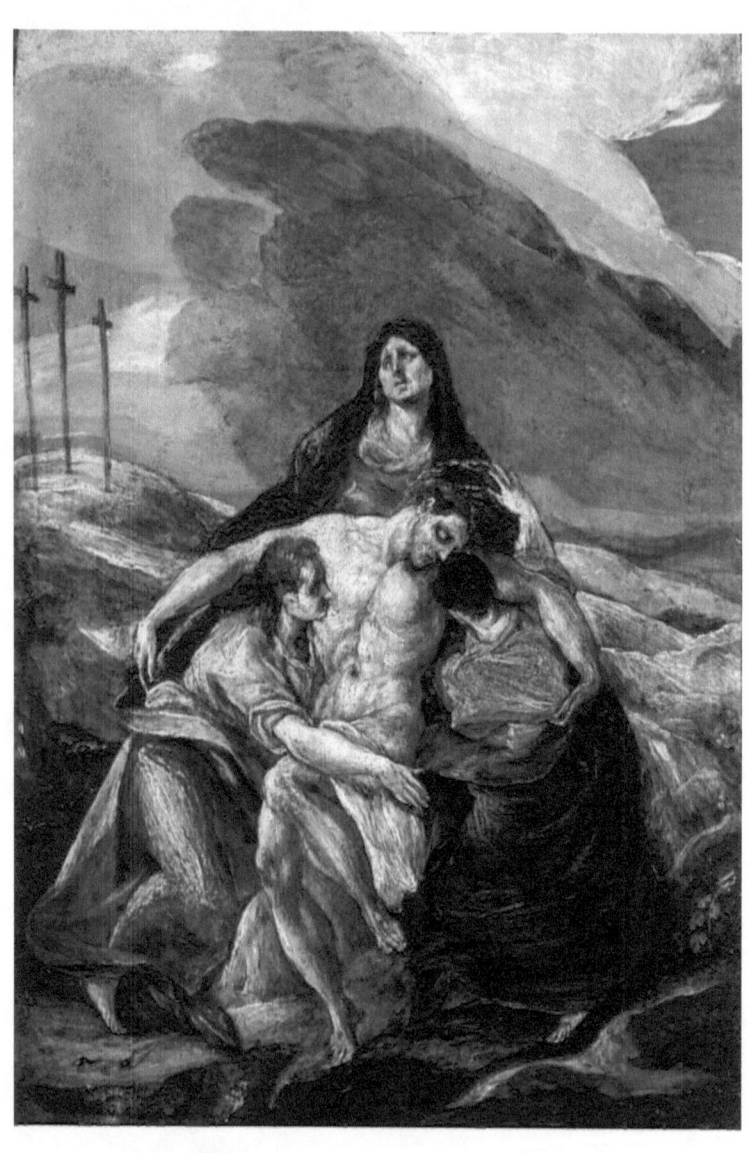

Pietà (The Lamentation of Christ)
1571-76, Tempera on panel, 29 x 20 cm

A translation in paint of Michelangelo's late sculptured group of the Pietà in Florence Cathedral, at the time in Rome. The pattern and the feeling are the same. The figures of the Dead Christ, His Mother, Saint Mary Magdalene and Joseph of Arimathea make one compact group. Michelangelo achieved this by his new treatment of form; El Greco by paint, by employing broader, more continuous passages of colour. The more vivid colours of Rome combine with the richer palette of Venice to convey the intensity of expression demanded by the subject. The horizontal composition of Venice, more suited to a narrative type of subject than to the single image, is given up and is only very rarely found appropriate in Spain.

Michelangelo's Pietà group was not the only source on which El Greco drew: the arrangement of Christ's legs and his outspread arms, no less than the idea of viewing one of the two bearers of his body from the side and the other from behind, derive from Michelangelo's drawing for Vittoria Colonna, in which, as in El Greco's painting, the Virgin is placed behind and above Christ.

In the collection of the Hispanic Society of America is a larger version of the subject, unsigned, in oil on canvas, for which this may be a study. The subject is not repeated in Spain.

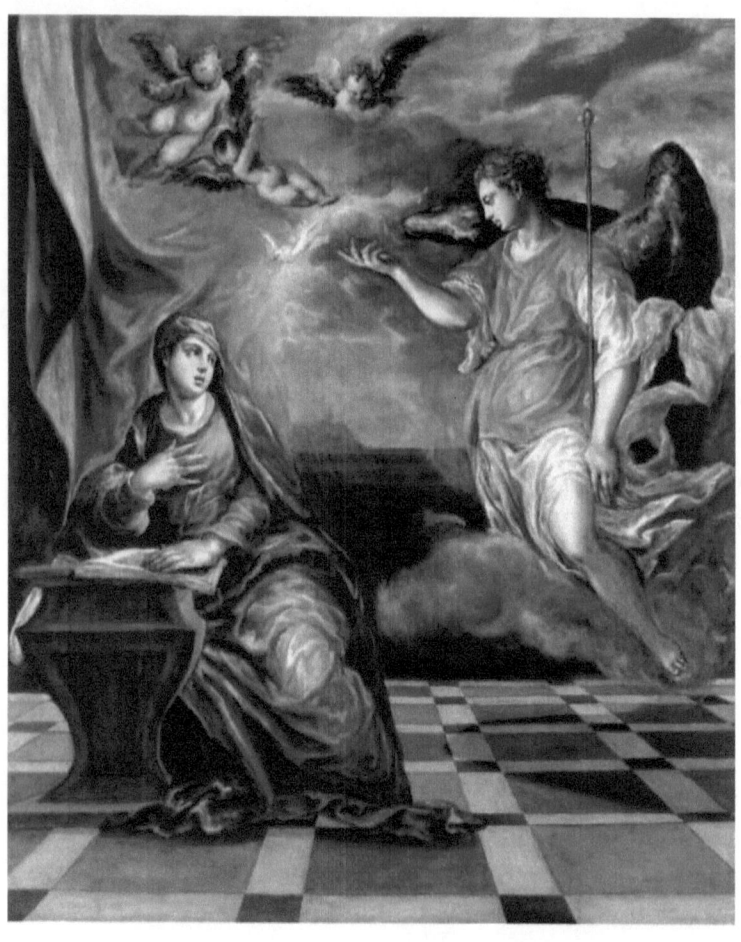

The Annunciation, c. 1576, Oil on canvas, 117 x 98 cm
This painting is the finest of El Greco's Italian
Annunciations, and in the clarity of its design, the
elegance of its poses and proportions and the
harmonious relationship of its figures and setting is
perhaps his most fully resolved picture in the Italian
manner.

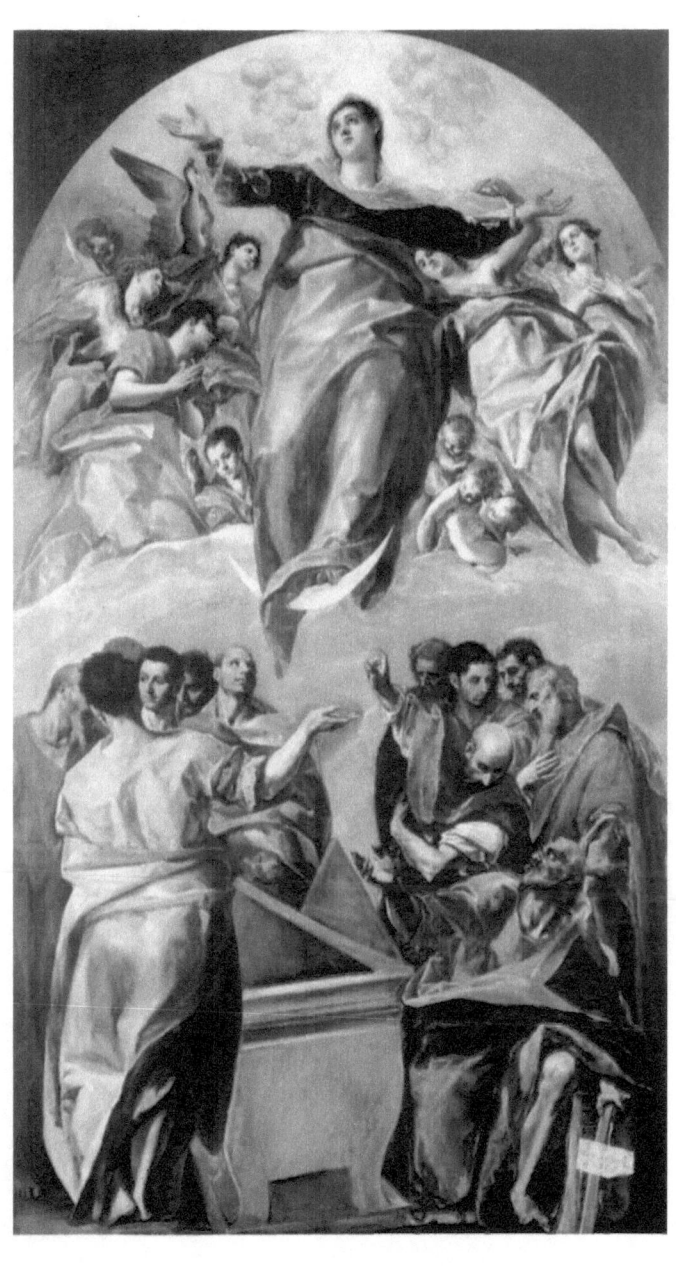

The Assumption of the Virgin, 1577, Oil on canvas, 401 x 229 cm

This, the first work executed in Spain, is the only painting by El Greco bearing the date of its execution. It is the first large-scale painting by his hand. There is a clear reminiscence of Venetian paintings of the subject, and specifically of Titian's early masterpiece in the church of the Frari in Venice, but the treatment is his own. The Virgin rises as from a chalice formed by the two unified groups on either side of the open tomb, which introduce and extend motifs developed in his Cleansing of the Temple and Healing of the Blind. A complete unity is achieved in this bipartite composition, in which the circle of Apostles, with its contained and concentrated internal movement, or emotion, is continued in the circle of angels with their easy and sympathetic movement around the rising figure of the Virgin. There is a sustained rhythm of the expressions, gestures and surface treatment within each group, and an easy and inevitable connection of one group with another. This is achieved essentially by paint, the measured relationship of the passages of color over the surface. This also explains his treatment of the draperies, which has its own logic, has no suggestion of conflict, but is also not concerned with disclosing the anatomy beneath.

When we compare the The Assumption of the Virgin with the famous painting on the same subject by Titian in the Frari Church in Venice, it becomes clear how new the paths El Greco took in Spain were. Under the influence of Michelangelo he not only found an unusually naturalistic style with monumental figures, but adopted a palette tending towards that of the Roman school. The great luminosity of the painting is striking, an illumination that, probably not coincidentally, conforms to the real light falling on it from above.

No other version of the subject is known, but the painting may be regarded as the forerunner of the related composition of the Immaculate Conception, a subject more compatible with El Greco's mystical approach to the Universe

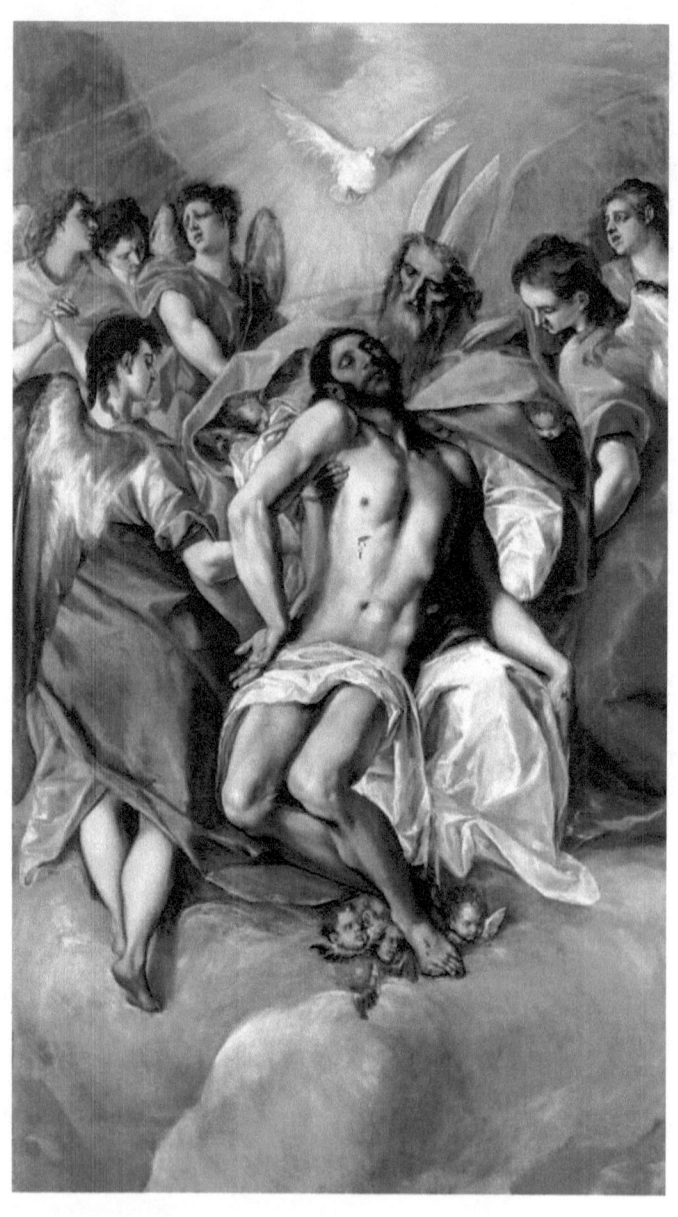

The Trinity, 1577, Oil on canvas, 300 x 179 cm

Here the reference is to Rome, rather than to Venice, and specifically to Michelangelo, developing the motif of the Pietà. The general scheme of the composition of the Trinity, however, refers to Dьrer's engraving of the same subject. The composition continues that of the Assumption below, slowing down the upward movement which finally comes to rest in the supported shoulders of Christ. Form is more in evidence here than in the Assumption, especially in the Michelangelesque motif of the naked Christ (for which the artist probably drew inspiration from Michelangelo's Pietà for Vittoria Colonna), and it is only later that he treats his figures with the same freedom as draperies. Here the suggestion of weight in the supported Dead Christ is appropriate. The stress on the dead body of Christ, together with the clamorous mannerist colors and the rather loose composition of the figures, produces a feverish pathos. El Greco was not to repeat this subject.

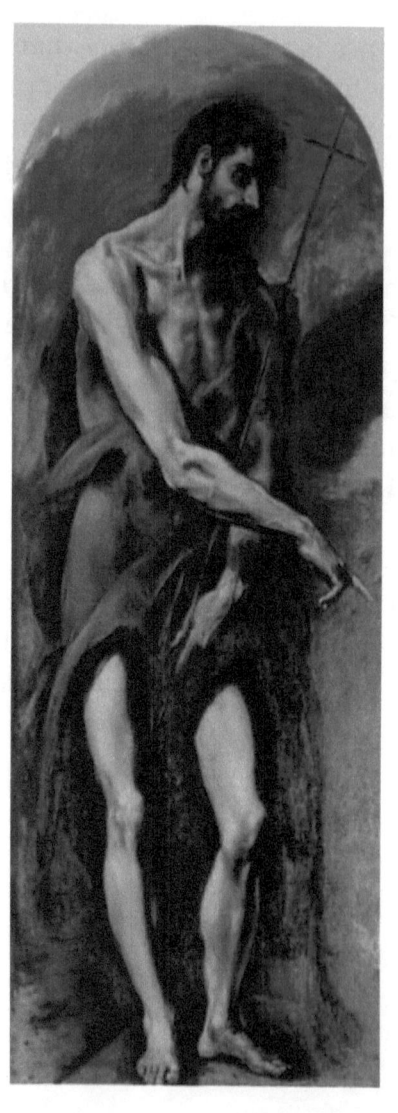

St John the Baptist, 1577-79, Oil on canvas, 212 x 78 cm

The figures of St John the Baptist and St John the
Evangelist flank the central large painting of The
Assumption on the High Altar in the church of Santo
Domingo el Antiguo in Tole

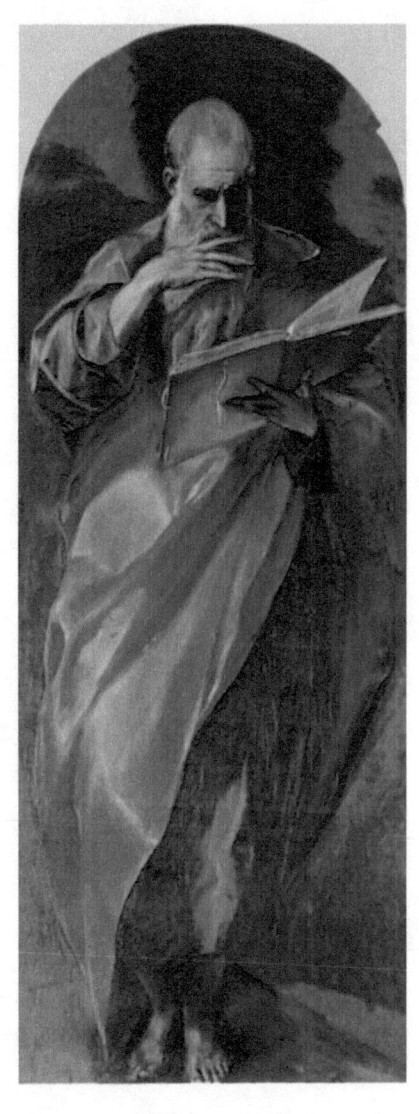

St John the Evangelist, 1577-79, Oil on canvas, 212 x 78 cm

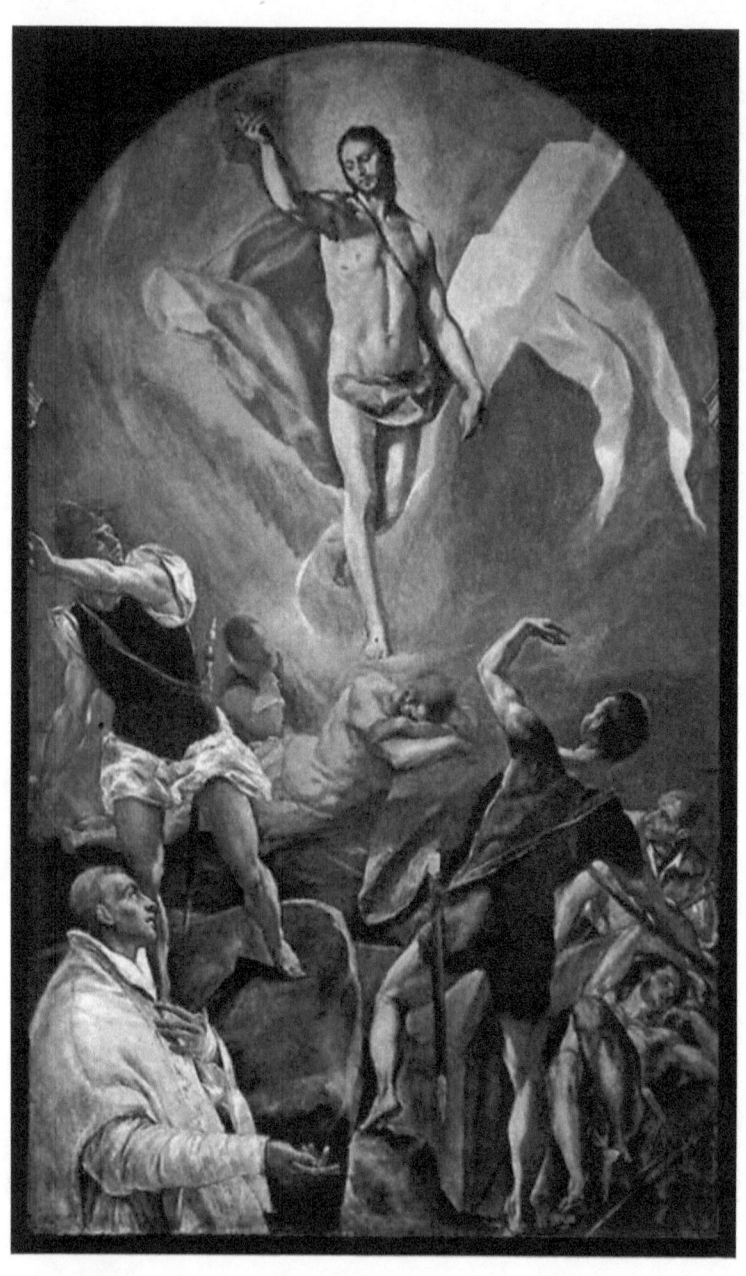

The Resurrection, 1577-79, Oil on canvas, 210 x 128 cm

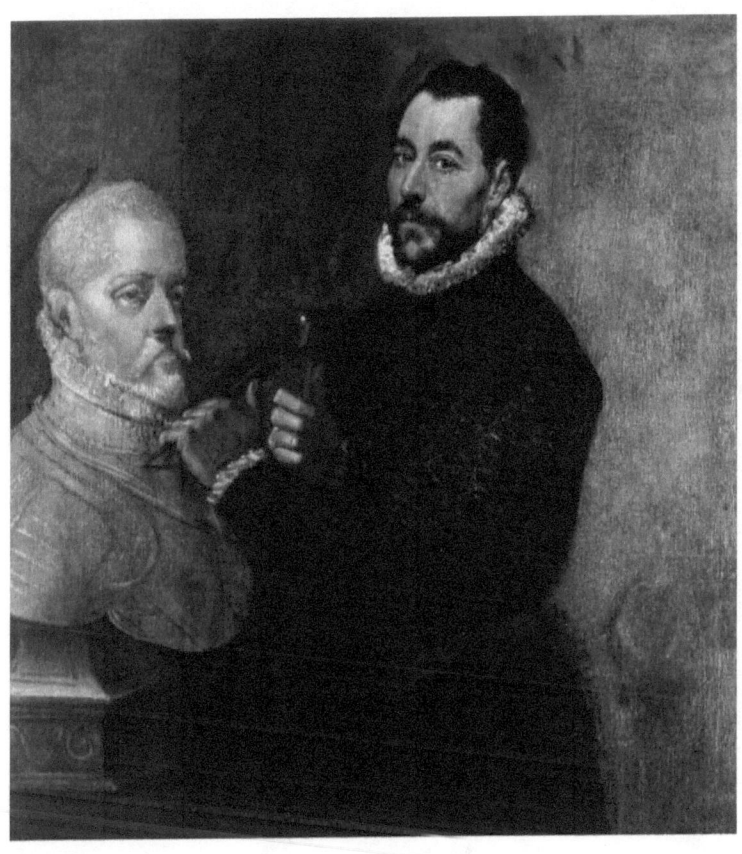

Portrait of a Sculptor, 1576-78, Oil on canvas, 94 x 87 cm
The problem of identification surrounds this portrait,
usually identified as the famous sculptor Pompeo
Leoni, the major sculptor at the court of Philip II, the
son of Leone Leoni, who had been employed in a
similar capacity by Philip's father, Charles V. A serious
objection to this identification is the fact that the marble
bust of Philip II included in the painting is significantly
different from those attributable to Leoni.

The sitter is depicted as a practitioner of a liberal art. He is elegantly and modestly dressed in black. His dark, penetrating eyes and high brow imply his intellectual capacity. The hammer is poised to suggest his mental deliberation. El Greco has ingeniously applied the conventional formula of the self-portrait, in which the artist turns to face the viewer while working at the easel. Wittily, the viewer can imagine the sculptor looking at the sitter (Philip II) posing for his bust portrait.

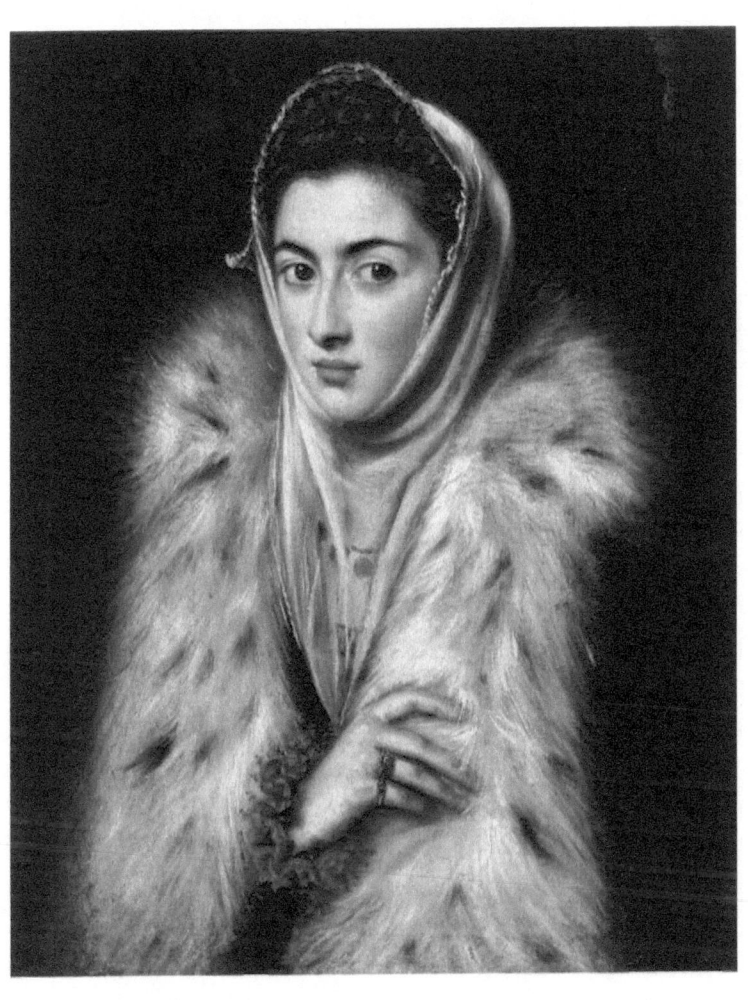

A Lady in a Fur Wrap, 1577-80, Oil on canvas, 62 x 59 cm

This is probably the earliest extant portrait which El Greco painted in Toledo. The treatment, with the greater continuity of brushstroke, is related to that of his portrait of Vincenzo Anastagi of his last years in Italy, and to his first paintings in Spain. In the manner of Titian, the lynx fur is freely and vigorously painted. The dark tafts have been cleverly arranged so that they seem to splay out from the sitter, thereby enhancing and vivifying her. The identity of the sitter is not known, but clearly the portrait is too informal and intimate for a sitter of royal or aristocratic blood. The fact that El Greco painted very few female portraits, the intimate quality of the portrait, the apparent age of the sitter, and the correspondence in time with the setting up of the household, lead some critics to the conclusion that this is a portrait of Jerynima de las Cuevas, his life-long companion in Spain, and the mother of his son, Jorge Manuel. Since evidence for Jerynima's appearance is completely lacking there have been more reasoned proposals on the basis of comparison with other portraits. However, these identifications present problems of their own.

Regarding the authorship of the painting, several other attributions have been put forward. It has been proposed as a work of Tintoretto, of an artist in the circle of the court painter Alonso Sónchez Coello, and most recently, of the Cremonese portrait painter Sofonisba Anguissola. None of these is any more convincing, however, than the traditional attribution.

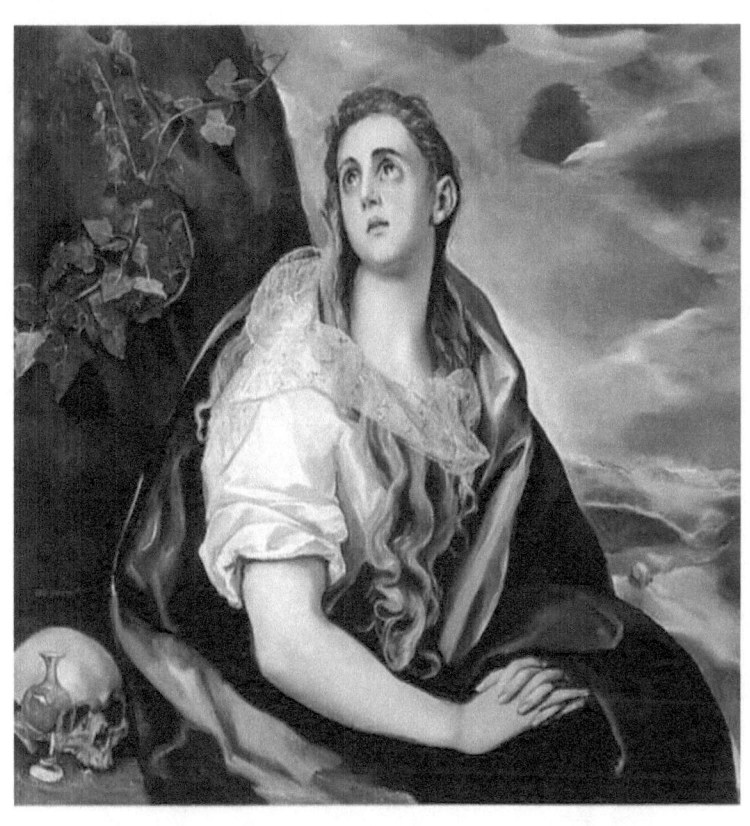

Penitent Mary Magdalene 1578, oil on canvas

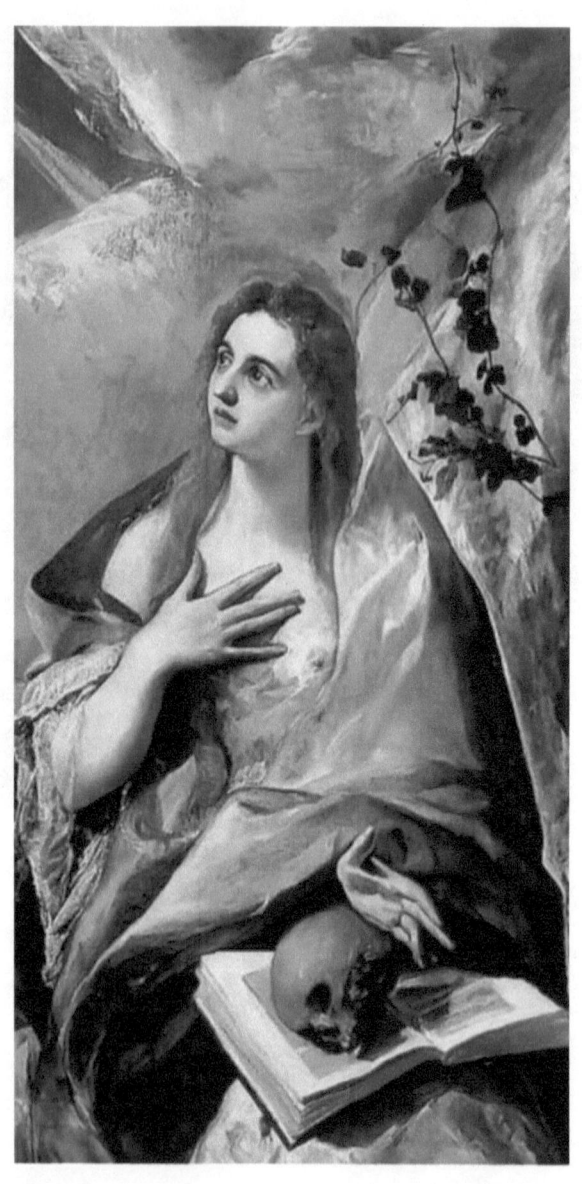

Mary Magdalene, 1578, oil on canvas

Portrayed as a hermit saint, Mary Magdalen sits alone outside her cave, which according to legend was at St-Baume in southern France. During the course of his career El Greco developed five different compositions representing the Magdalen in penitence. This is an excellent example of the first of these developed soon after his arrival in Spain. Demand for such images was so strong that El Greco had copies made in his workshop from his originals. In this painting, the refined execution of the drapery and of the still-life indicates the hand of El Greco himself. In this composition El Greco drew on Titian's interpretation of the subject in a painting now in the Hermitage. However, El Greco's rendition is more emotionally charged. A later version of the same composition in the Nelson Atkins Museum, Kansas City shows the Magdalen in exactly the same position but with the landscape to the left and the still-life to the right.

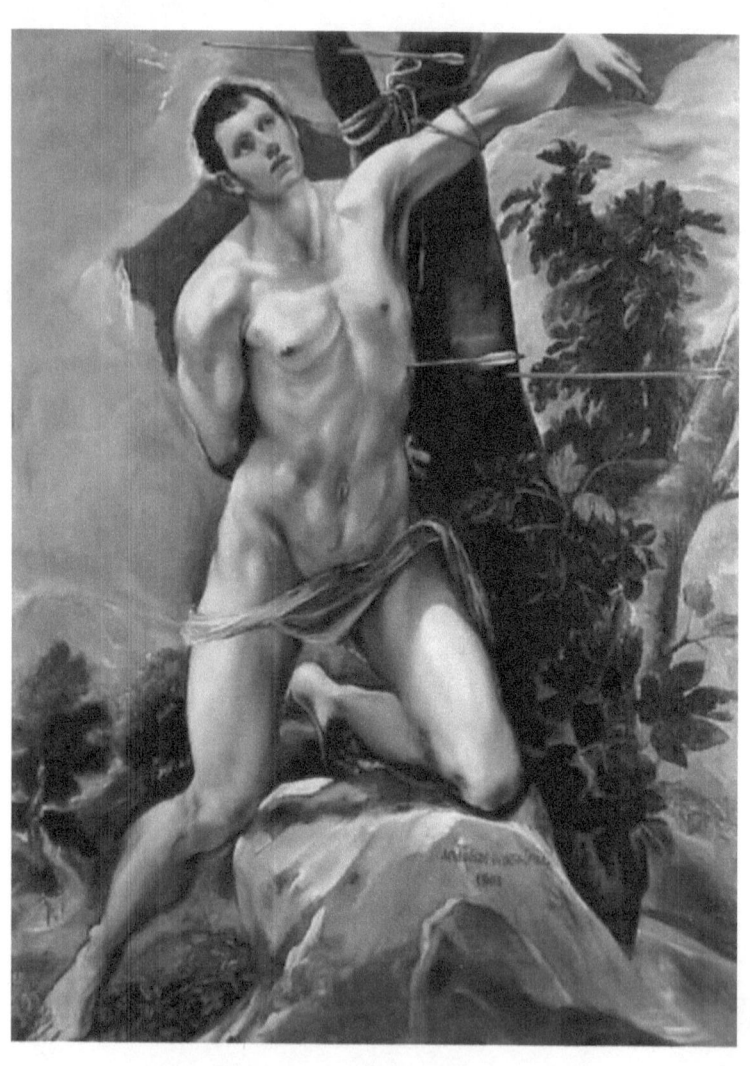

St. Sebastian, 1578, oil on canvas

The St Sebastian is El Greco's first life-size male nude, and it is one of the key works of the artist's first years in Spain. The Saint abandoned after his martyrdom and presumed death. The style is that of around 1580. The frontal placing of the nude figure and treatment of the forms avoids a three-dimensional emphasis. The greater prominence of the setting - and of actual depth, in the vista on the right - compared with the paintings for Santo Domingo, the Cathedral and the Escorial, depends on the subject. In comparable representations of Saints, as of the Magdalene or Saint Jerome in the wilderness, he continues to indicate a setting. Where the image alone is demanded, as in his series of Apostles, a setting is omitted. In this painting the forms of tree and rock and the silhouette of the foliage are made to continue the plane of the figure. It is perhaps the natural sequence in the process of dematerialisation that the more flexible elements, the draperies, preceded the nude figure and natural forms. El Greco did not use the pose again for a Saint Sebastian. A related figure is the Christ in the Prado Baptism of some fifteen to twenty years later; the Saint Jerome of his last year shows the culmination of this development. The compositional motif of the pose, with the outstretched leg taking the movement upwards appears in the Adoration of the Shepherds of similar date, and indeed in El Greco's work is first met in the Adoration of the Modena Triptych.

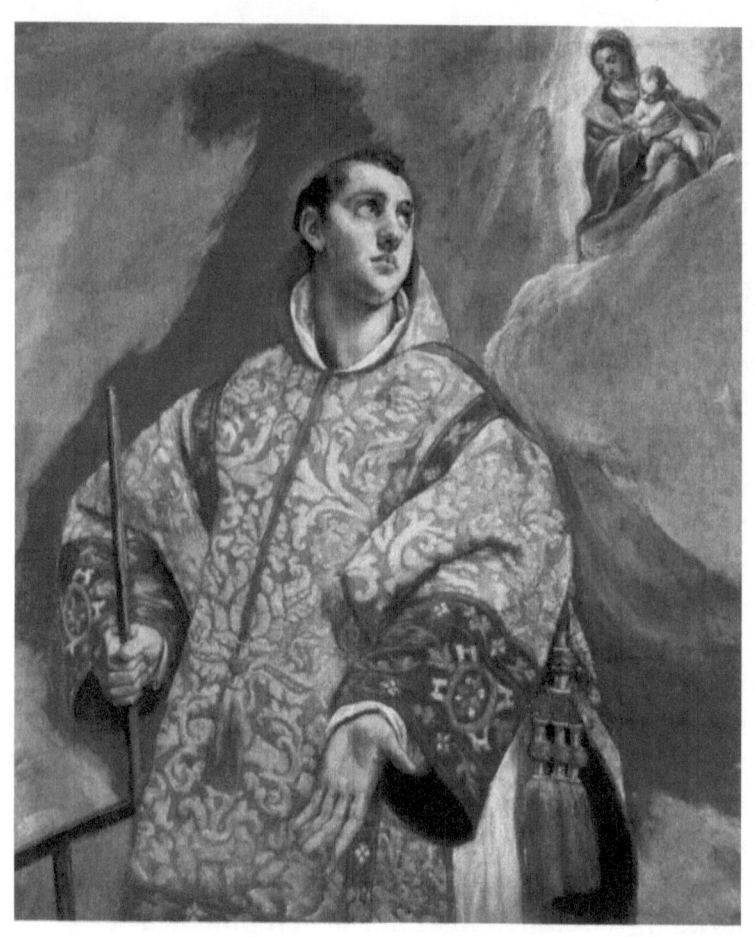

Apparition of the Virgin to St Lawrence, 1578-80, Oil on canvas, 119 x 102 cm

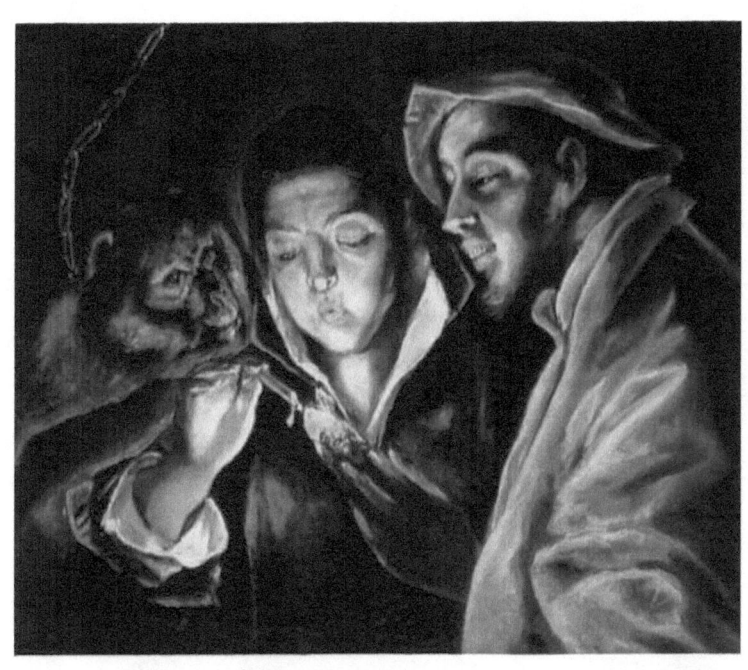

Allegory with a fool, monkey and boy, inflaming a
candle with charcoal, 1579, oil on canvas

The central figure is closely based on El Greco's earlier
painting of a Boy Blowing on an Ember in Naples but
the scene has been enlarged to include another male
figure, wearing a yellow jacket and red cap, and a
chained monkey, who emerges from the darkness on
the left to look over the boy's shoulder. The
composition, known in two other autograph versions
(one of similar size in Edinburgh from around 1590,
and another smaller and later in the Prado from around
1600), has usually been interpreted as an allegory with
some sort of moralising intent; it is unlikely that it was
conceived simply as a genre scene. It bears the
traditional title 'Fόbula', meaning fable or story.

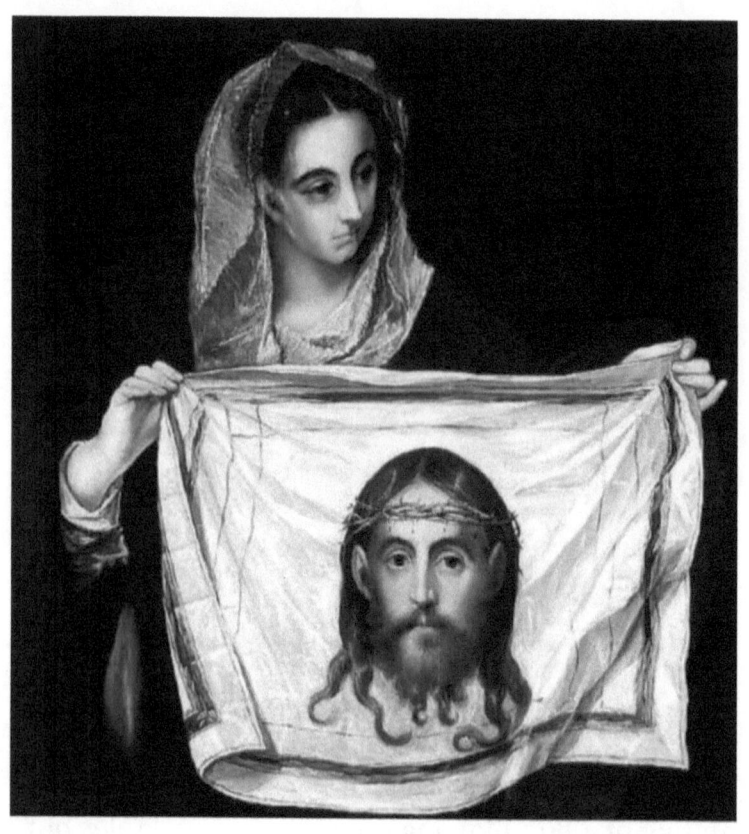

The veil of St. Veronica, 1580, oil on canvas
El Greco treated the theme of the veil of Veronica
several times. This version is one of El Greco's
important paintings of the period. The artist used the
same model as for one of the Marys in the Disrobing (El
Espolio), but the degree of naturalism varies
considerably in these two contemporary renderings.

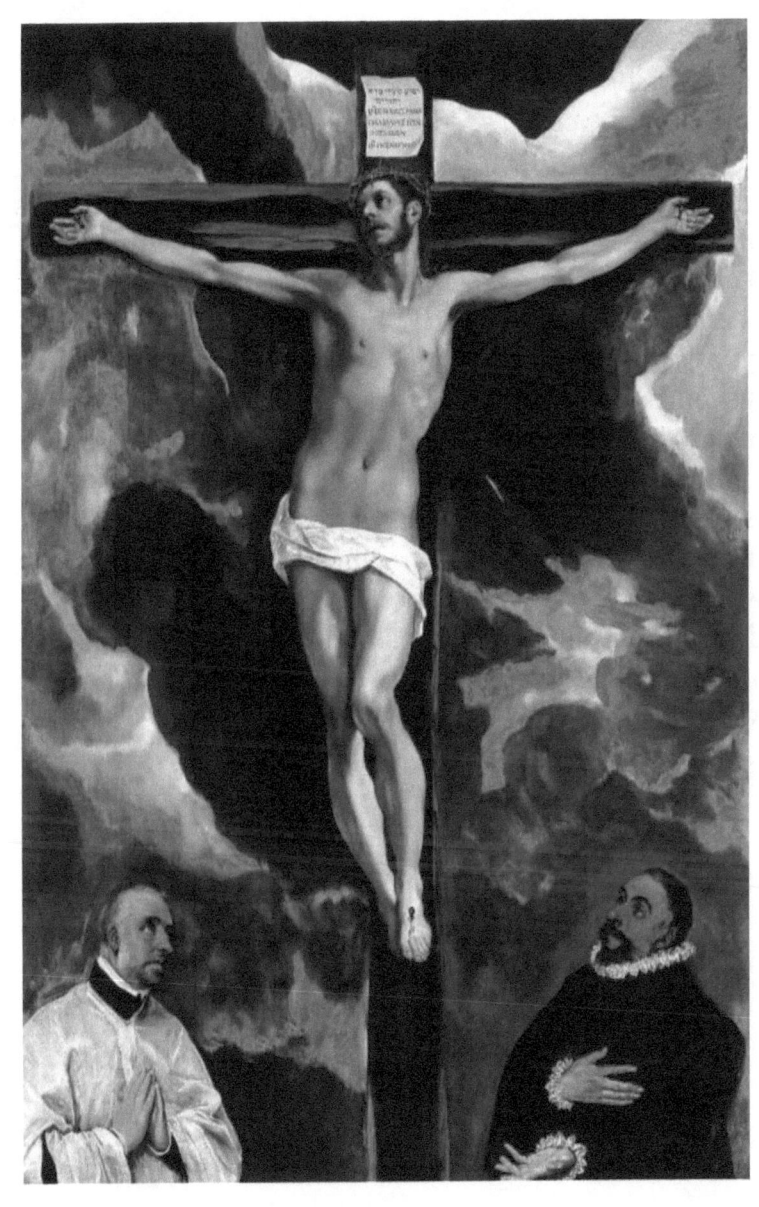

Christ on the Cross Adored by Two Donors, c. 1580, Oil
on canvas, 248 x 180 cm

A priest and a nobleman, probably the patrons who commissioned the painting, are shown praying before Christ on the cross. (It is assumed by some scholars that they are the brothers Diego and Antonio Covarrubias.) El Greco has included realistic details such as the drops of blood trickling from Christ's forehead, hands and feet, while leaving his torso and legs unstained. Light and shadow model Christ's musculature, the elongation of his contorted body enhancing a sense of his suffering. Above his head a sheet of paper stuck to the cross informs us in Hebrew, Greek and Latin that he is Jesus of Nazareth, with the additional ironic words in Greek hailing him as the King of Jews. The influence of Michelangelo - whose works El Greco would have known in Rome - is recognized in the depiction of the naked Christ. In fact, the posture and anatomy of El Greco's Christ echo in reverse Michelangelo's drawing for Vittoria Colonna.

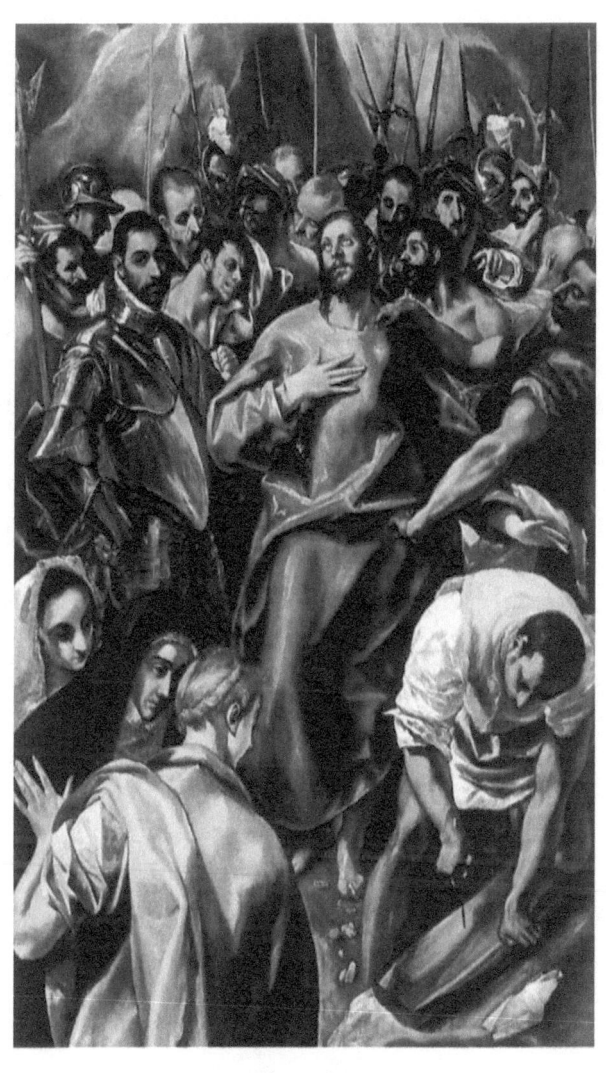

The Disrobing of Christ, 1583-84, Oil on canvas, 165 x
99 cm

This canvas is one of three versions which El Greco painted of the subject. The impression of the artist's Venetian years, and particularly the works of Titian, can still be felt in the strictly centralized composition, in the relatively plastic modelling of the figures, and above all in the sophistication of the the palette. The way in which the figures below left are sliced by the frame, and the slight foreshortening empolyed in the figure of Christ, who appears to be leaning backwards into the picture, suggest that the canvas was destined to be hung at some height. If we consider in this regard the luminous red of Christ's robe, by which he is made to stand out from the crowd, and the multiple verticals of the figures and lances, the painting seems to point beyond its immediate subject to the coming ascension.

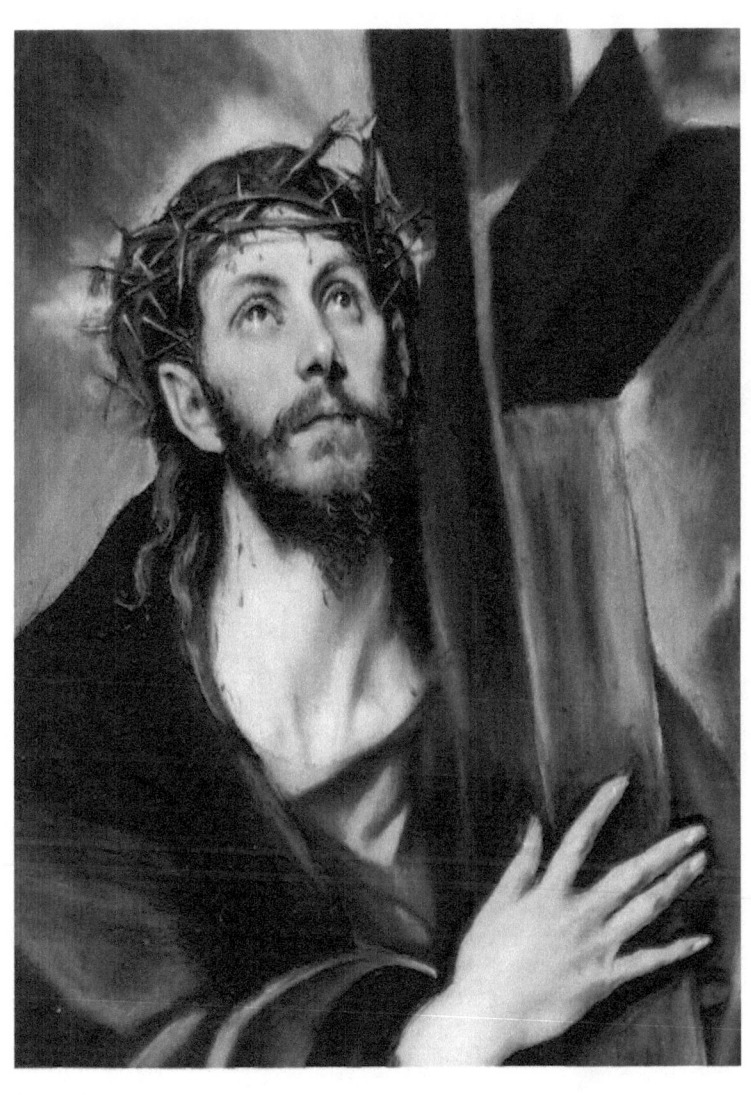

Christ Carrying the Cross (detail), 1580s, Oil on canvas

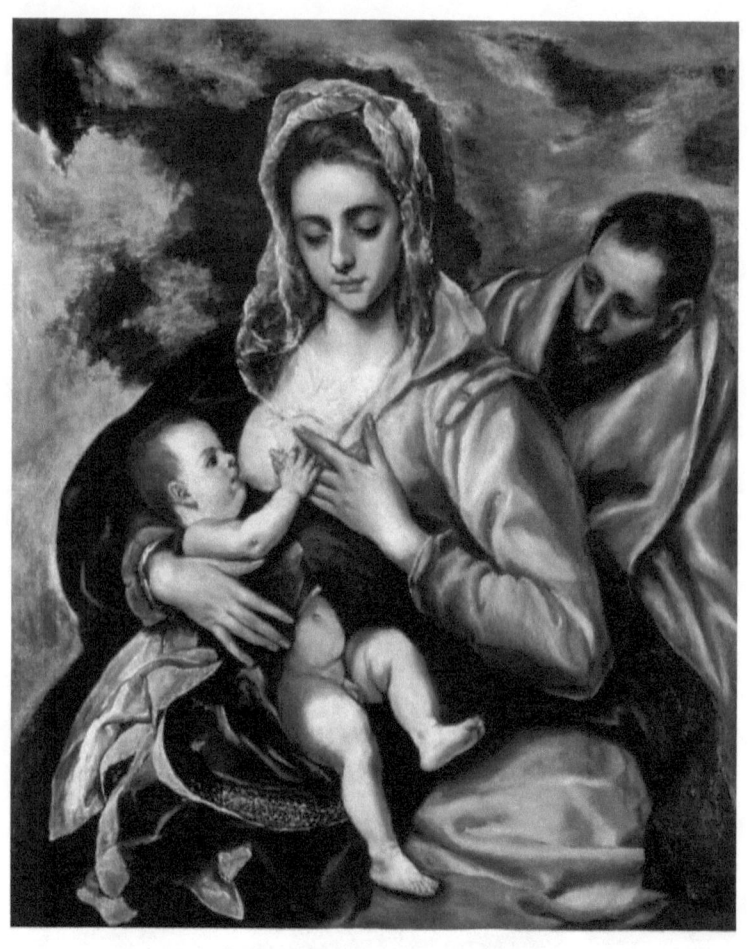

The Holy Family, c. 1585, Oil on canvas, 106 x 87,5 cm

It was only after El Greco moved to Spain that he treated the theme of the Madonna and Child in both half-length and full-length format, however, he invariably included St Joseph, in keeping with the new prominence the saint was given in Counter-Reformation theology. The painting of the Hispanic Society of America is one of El Greco's finest paintings and his earliest treatment of the theme. It served as the point of departure for a larger canvas in the Hospital of St John the Baptist in Toledo (Tavera Hospital), in which the composition was enriched by the inclusion of St Anne to the left of the Virgin.

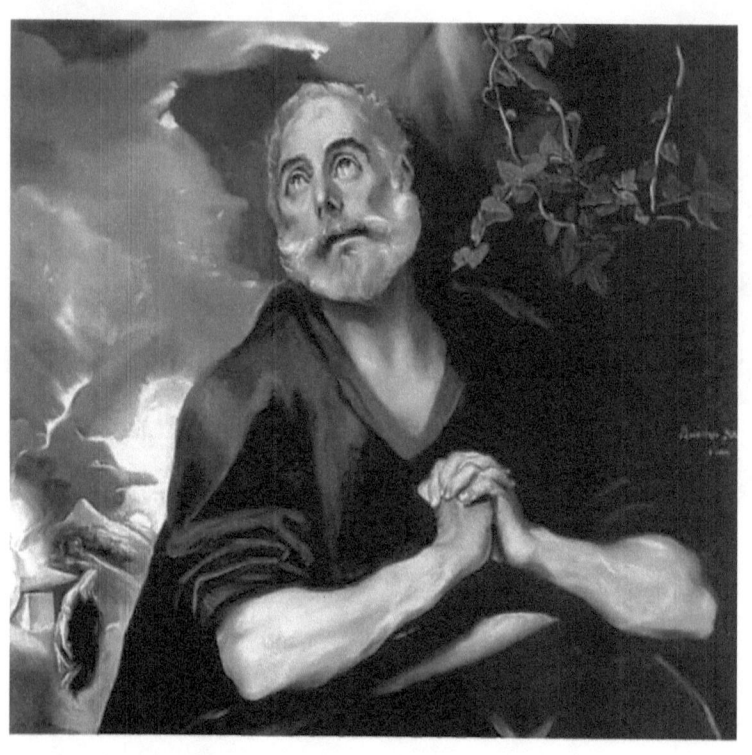

Penitence of St. Peter (detail), 1586, oil on canvas

This is the earliest version of a subject El Greco painted in at least six different autograph variants (several of which gave rise to studio copies) over the course of his career in Spain. He made the subject, which was new in the Counter-Reformation period, one of his specialities. In this painting St Peter raises his tear-filled eyes to Heaven, his hands joined in prayer. The background scene of visional qualities on the left represents the Magdalen returning from the empty tomb after receiving the announcement of Christ's resurrection from an angel. St Peter appears a great number of times in El Greco's oeuvre and he is depicted with remarkable consistency. The saint is always shown with white hair and beard, and he often wears his yellow cloak over a blue tunic.

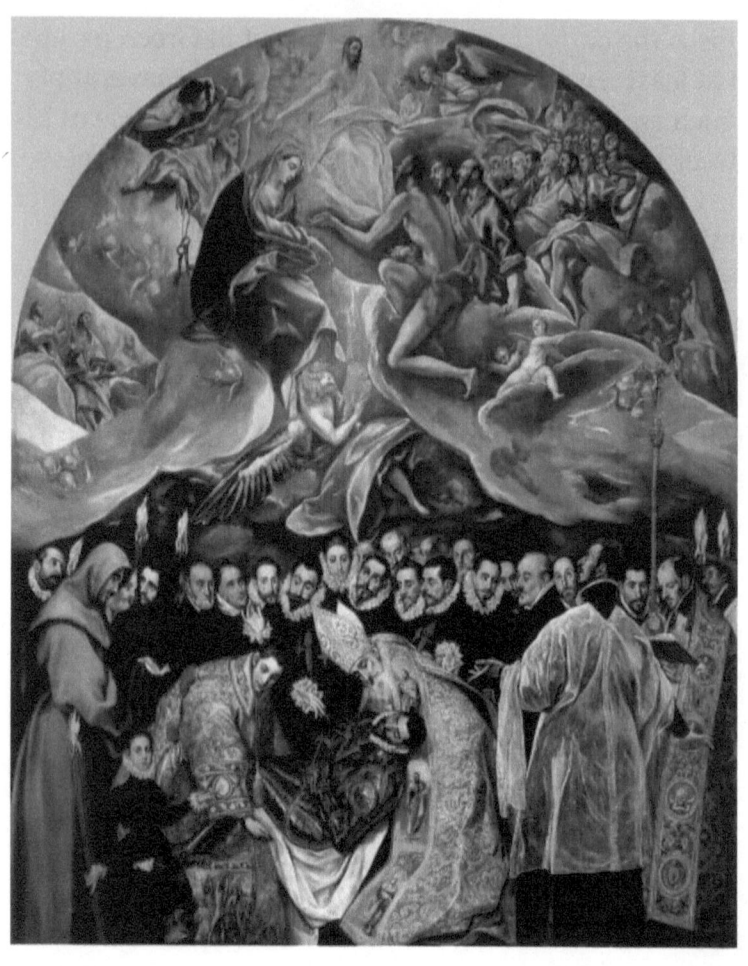

The Burial of the Count of Orgaz, 1586-88, Oil on
canvas, 480 x 360 cm

The contract for the painting is dated 18th March 1586.
El Greco agreed to finish the painting by Christmas of
the same year. This commission again resulted in
litigation over the valuation, the final outcome of which
was that the artist accepted the amount of the original
valuation, 1200 ducados.

The painting illustrates a popular local legend. In 1312, a certain Don Gonzalo Ruнz, native of Toledo, and Señor of the town of Orgaz, died (the family received the title of Count, by which he is generally known, only later). He was a pious man who, among other charitable acts, left moneys for the enlargement and adornment of the church of Santo Tomй (El Greco's parish church). At his burial, Saint Stephen and Saint Augustine intervened to lay him to rest. The occasion for the commission of the painting for the chapel in which the Señor was buried, was the resumption of the tribute payable to the church by the town of Orgaz, which had been withheld for over two centuries.

The painting remains in the chapel - the actual scene of the event - for which it was ordered. Already in 1588, people flocked to see the painting. This immediate popular reception depended, however, on the 'life-like portrayal of the notable men of Toledo of the time'. Indeed, this painting is sufficient to rank El Greco among the few great portrait painters. Nowadays the painting can communicate to us a whole society and age, as perhaps no other single work of art can, and at the same time offer us one of the great marvels of painting.

It was the custom for the eminent and noble men of the town to assist at the burial of the high-born, and it was stipulated in the contract that the scene should be represented in this way. Without the contemporary confirmation, it would be clear that all are portraits. Unfortunately, there is no record of the identity of the sitters. Andrūs Nъñez, the parish priest, and a friend of El Greco's, who was responsible for the commission, is certainly the figure on the extreme right. The artist himself can be recognised in the caballero third from the left, immediately above the head of Saint Stephen. The artist's son acts as the young page. The signature of the artist appears on the handkerchief in the pocket of the young boy, and by a strange conceit it is followed by the date '1578' - the year of Jorge Manuel's birth, and certainly not the date of the painting. The boy points to the body of the deceased, thus bringing together birth and death.

The painting is very clearly divided into two zones, the heavenly above and the terrestrial below, but there is little feeling of duality. The upper and lower zones are brought together compositionally. The grand circular mandorla-like pattern of the two Saints descended from Heaven echoes the pattern formed by the Virgin and Saint John the Baptist, and the action is given explicit expression. The point of equilibrium is the outstretched hand poised in the void between the two Saints, whence the mortal body descends, and the Soul, in the medieval form of a transparent and naked child, is taken up by the angel to be received in Heaven. The supernatural appearance of the Saints is enhanced by the splendour of colour and light of their gold vestments. The powerful cumulative emotion expressed by the group of participants is suffused and sustained through the composition by the splendour, variety and vitality of the colour and of light.

This is the first completely personal work by the artist. There are no longer any references to Roman or Venetian formulas or motifs. He has succeeded in eliminating any description of space. There is no ground, no horizon, no sky and no perspective. Accordingly, there is no conflict, and a convincing expression of a supernatural space is achieved. This is the beginning of his real development, and the process of dematerialisation and spiritualisation continues.

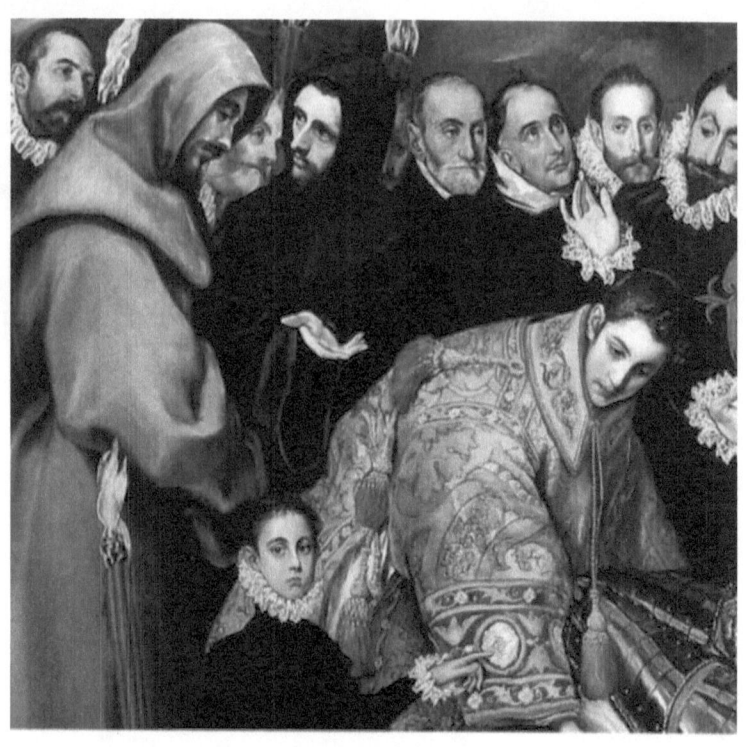

The Burial of the Count of Orgaz (detail), 1588, oil on canvas

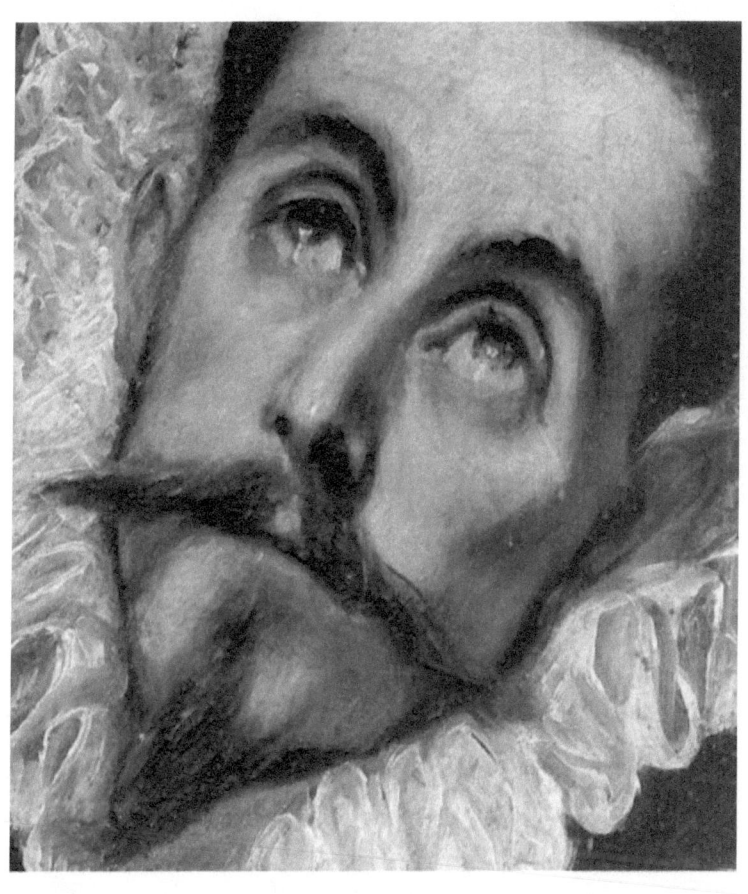

Burial of Count de Orgaz (detail), 1588, oil on canvas

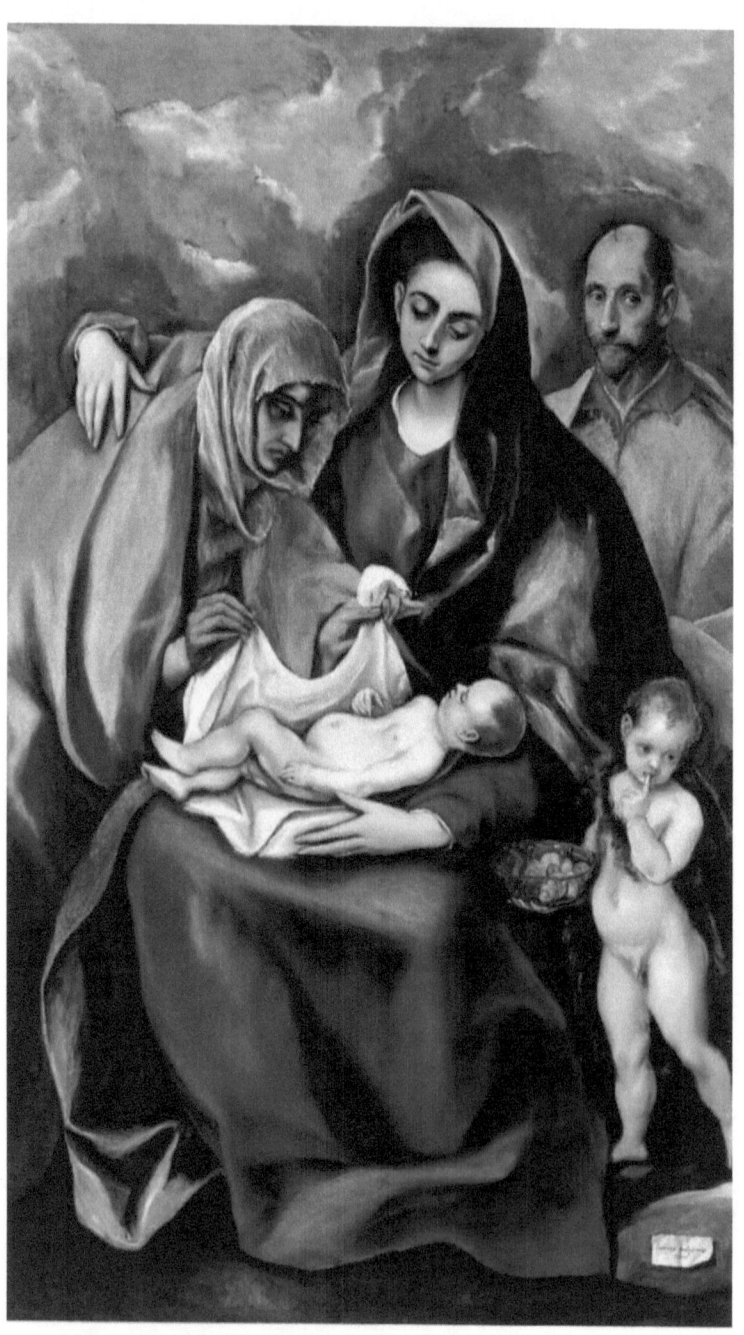

Holy Family, 1588, oil on canvas

It was only after El Greco moved to Spain that he treated the theme of the Madonna and Child in both half-length and full-length format, however, he invariably included St Joseph, in keeping with the new prominence the saint was given in Counter-Reformation theology. This painting from the Santa Leocadia in Toledo (presently on loan to the Museo de Santa Cruz) is El Greco's earliest version of the full-length depictions of the Holy Family. Two inferior paintings derive from it, a smaller version in the National Gallery of Art, Washington, and another in the Prado, Madrid. The primary difference between the Santa Leocadia version and the others is the substitution in those works of a conventional image of St Joseph for the balding figure that appears in this one. This figure is probably a portrait of the donor. It was painted out at one point and was only revealed by cleaning in 1981. Noteworthy is the figure of St John the Baptist: he turns towards the viewer and makes a gesture urging silence so that the child will not be awakened.

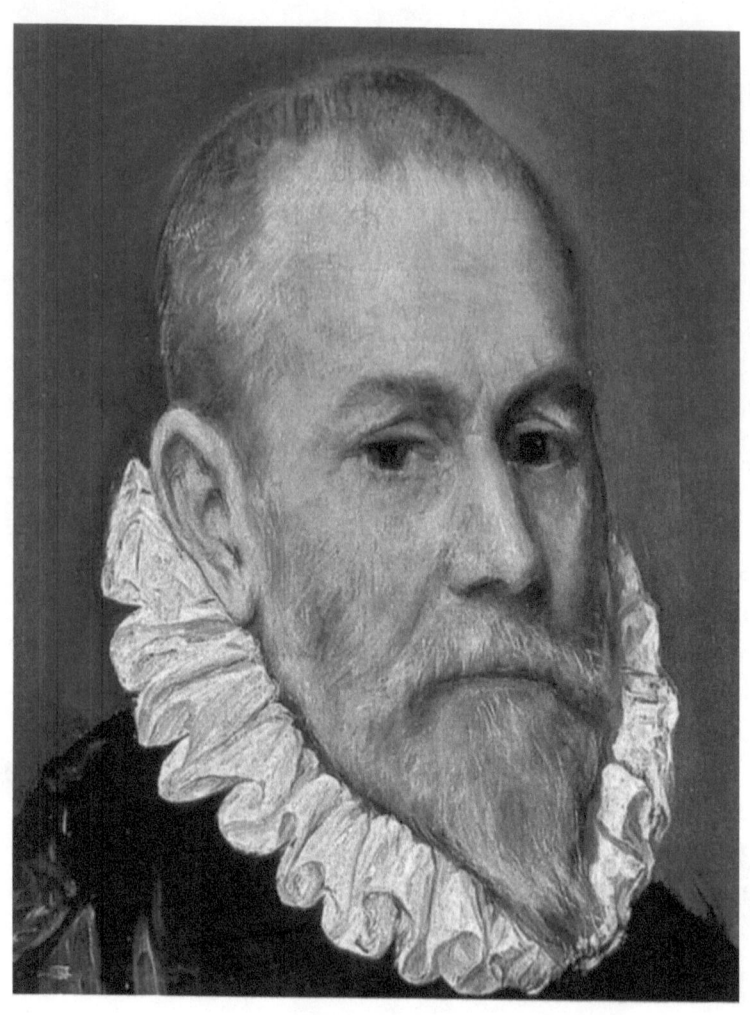

Doctor, 1588, oil on canvas

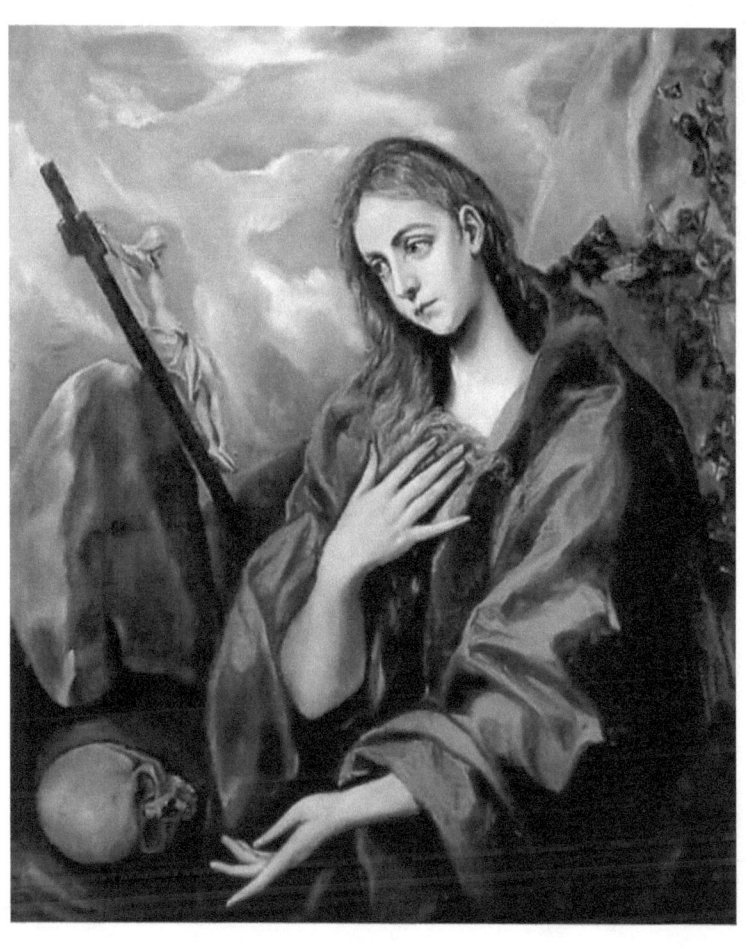

Penitence of Mary Magdalene, 1590, oil on canvas

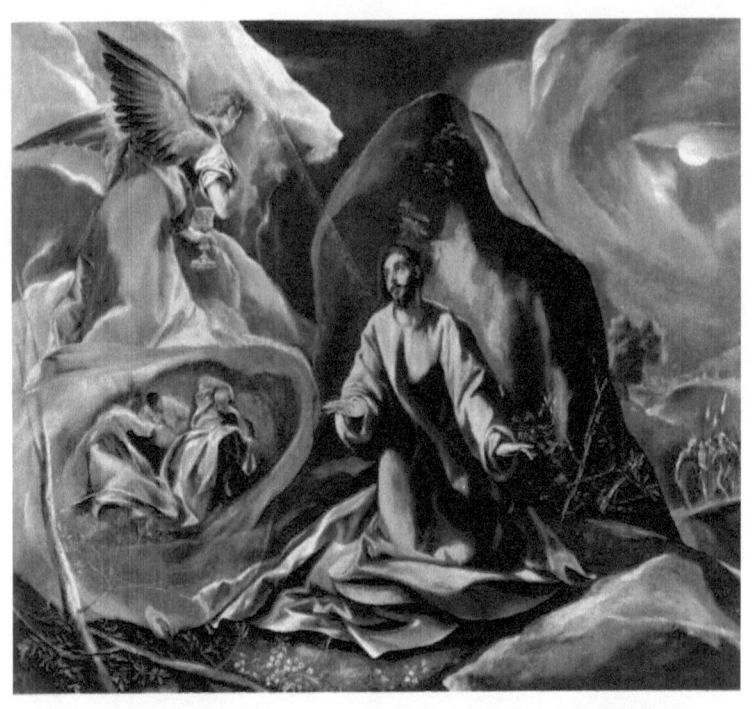

Agony in the Garden, 1590, oil on canvas

There are many versions of The Agony in the Garden painted by El Greco and his workshop; it was one of his most successful inventions. He painted the subject both as a horizontal and as a vertical composition. The version in the Ohio museum is probably the prototype, or at least the best autograph version of the horizontal type. The Agony in the Garden testifies to an astonishing development of the artist. The Italian influences recede to the same degree as El Greco frees himself from his obligation to nature. The figures lose their sense of substance, while their expressiveness is amplified by the unreal shapes assumed by the landscape. Thus Christ is literally heightened by the rock behind him, while the disciples are seen in a sheltering cave as a symbol of sleep. The figures are absolved from logical relationships of scale. The falling diagonal which leads from an angel, through Christ, to the soldiers on the right-hand edge of the painting is a visual statement of the inevitability of Christ's fate. Such departures from the natural model, also evident in the visionary apparition of the moon, were one of the major reasons for the revival of interest in El Greco's work around 1900.

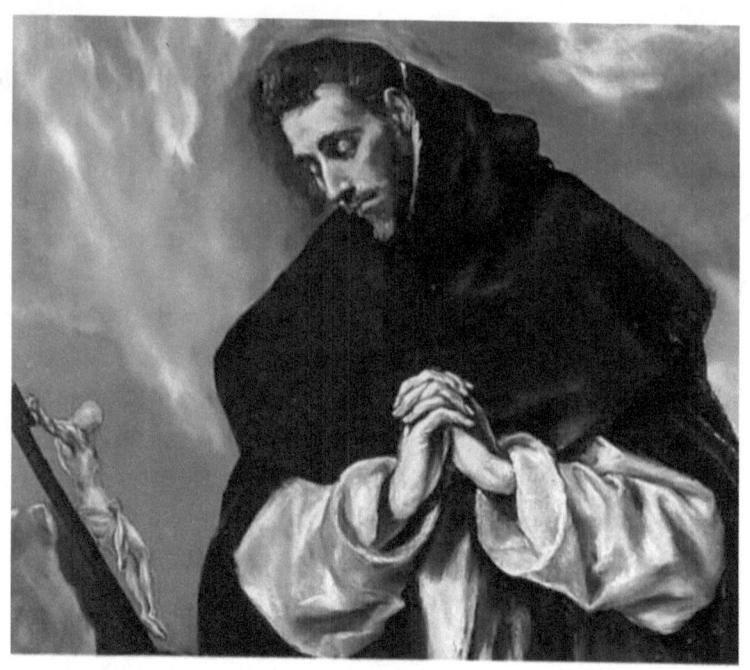

The prayer of St. Dominic (detail), 1590, oil on canvas
The painting represents the thirteenth-century founder
of the Dominican order kneeling in isolation on a rocky
plateau in prayerful devotion before a crucifix. Behind
him is a landscape with one of El Greco's haunting
skies filled with swirling, back-lit clouds. Considering
the individual features El Greco has given the saint, it is
assumed that the picture was based upon the features
of a particular person, someone the artist knew
personally. The crucifix, propped against the rocks, is
repeated by El Greco in a number of paintings showing
saints in devotion: he must have created a drawn or
painted model that he could refer to for replication.

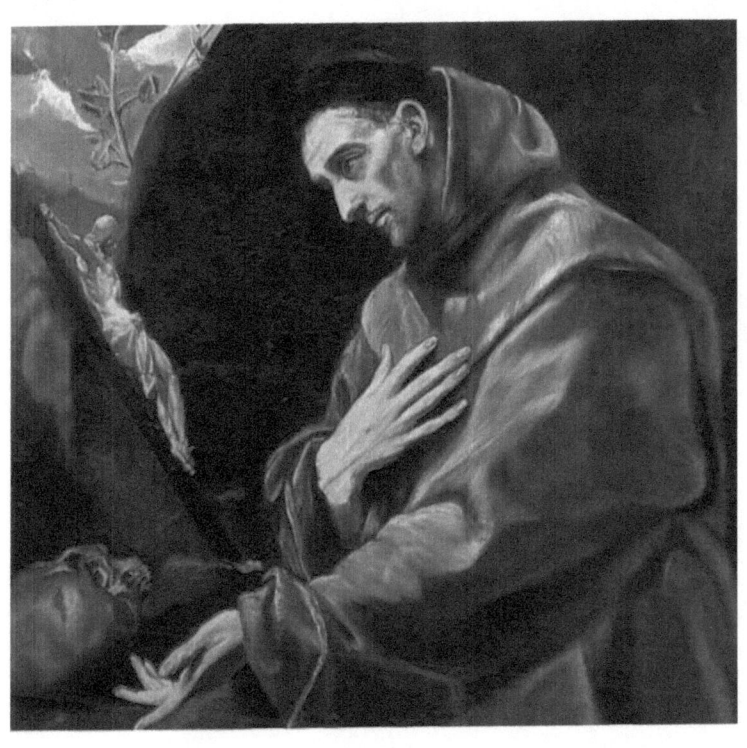

Prayer of St Francis (detail), 1590, oil on canvas

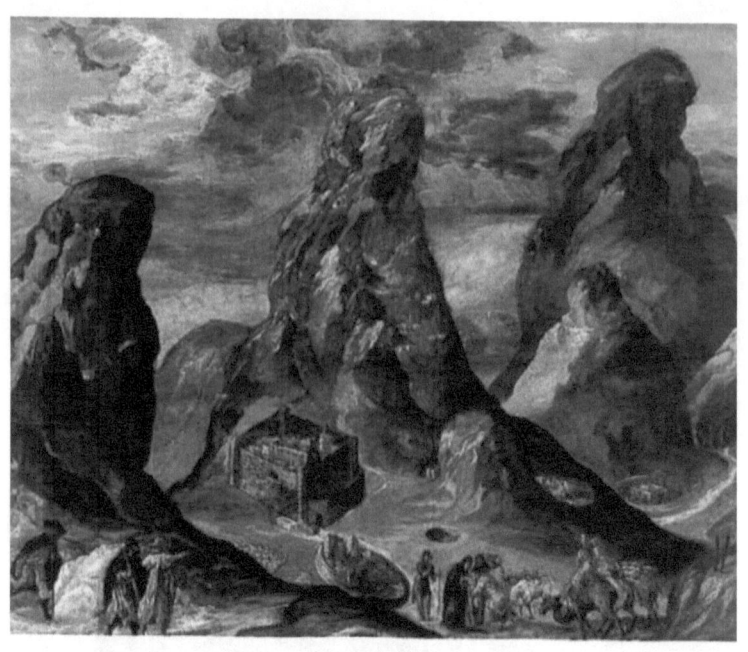

Sinai, 1592, oil on canvas

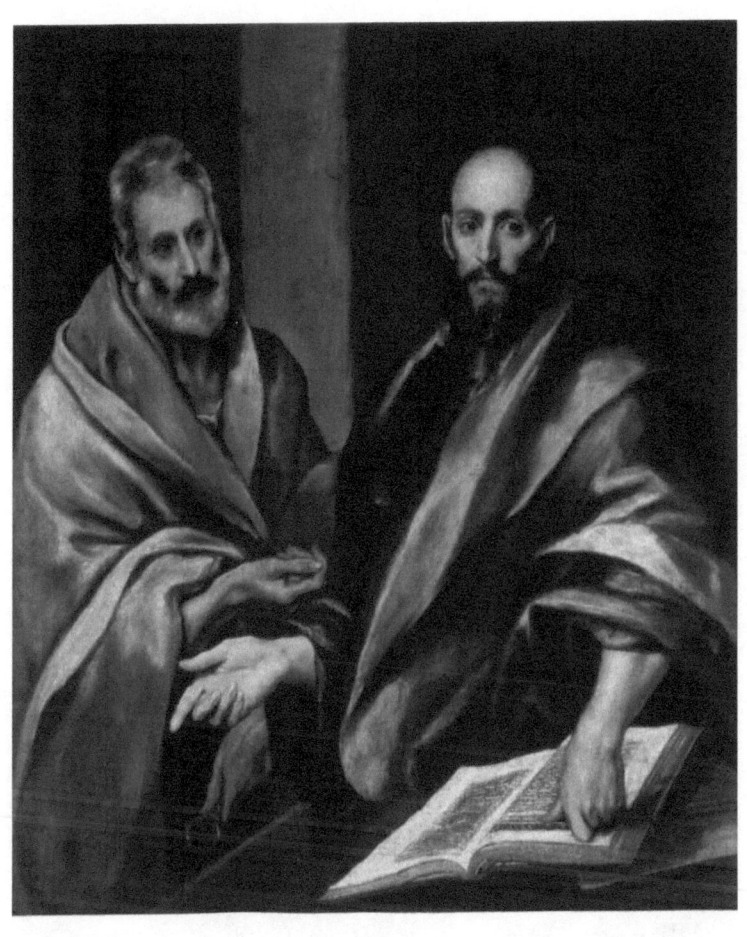

Apostles Peter and Paul, c. 1592, Oil on canvas, 121,5 x
105 cm

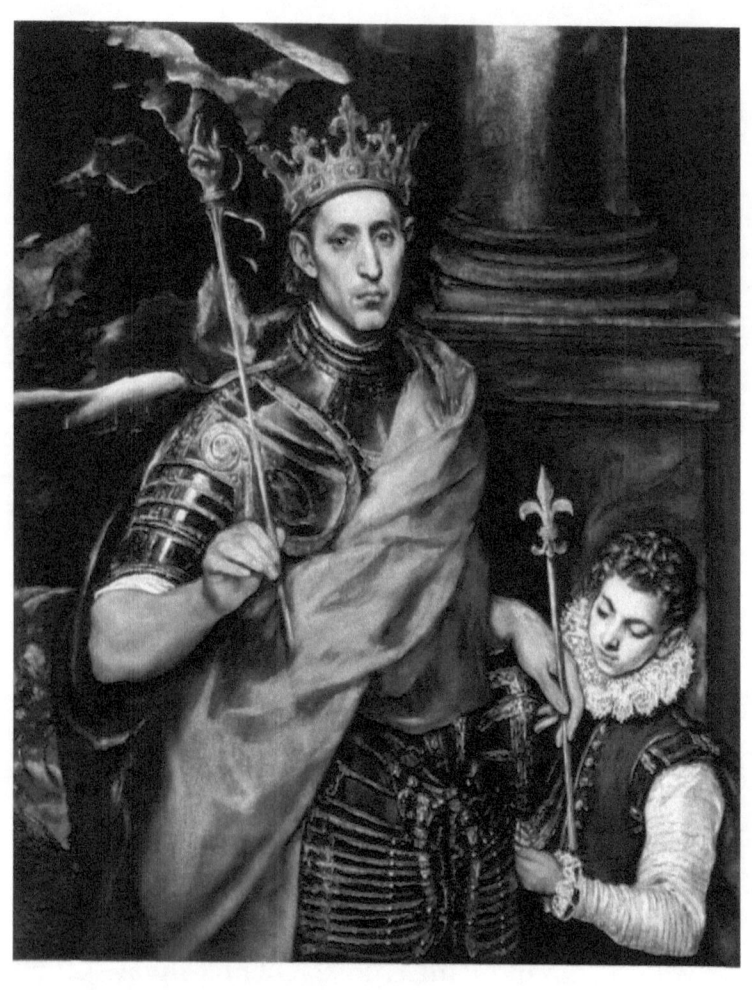

St Louis, King of France, with a Page, 1592-95, Oil on
canvas, 120 x 96 cm

The painting obviously represents a king, since all the royal attributes are present - crown, sceptre with fleur-de-lys, and 'main de justice'; he wears modern armour, except for the fact that the forearms are bare. The column, no doubt, symbolizes the might of the warrior. The night landscape under moonlit clouds in the background is reminiscent of El Greco's representations of Toledo in the late 1590s.

Various identifications of the principal figure have been made: Ferdinand V, the Catholic, King of Castile and Aragon, conqueror of Granada, who drove the Moors from Spain; St Louis, King of France; Ferdinand III, the saintly King of Castile and Leyn, famous for his victories over the Moors. Others regard it as a secular portrait representing a victorious king of Spain - a Visigothic king, one of the sovereigns already mentioned, or Alfonso VI of Castile and Leyn, the conqueror of Toledo in 1085. Presently it is accepted that the painting represents St Louis, King of France.

There is an inferior replica, without the page, in Madrid, it is attributed to El Greco's son.

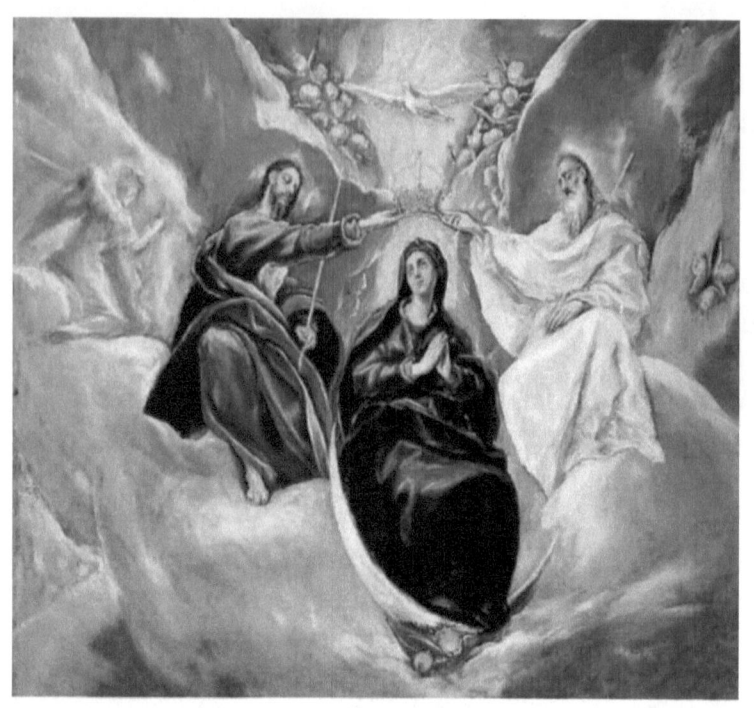

Coronation of the Virgin, 1592, oil on canvas

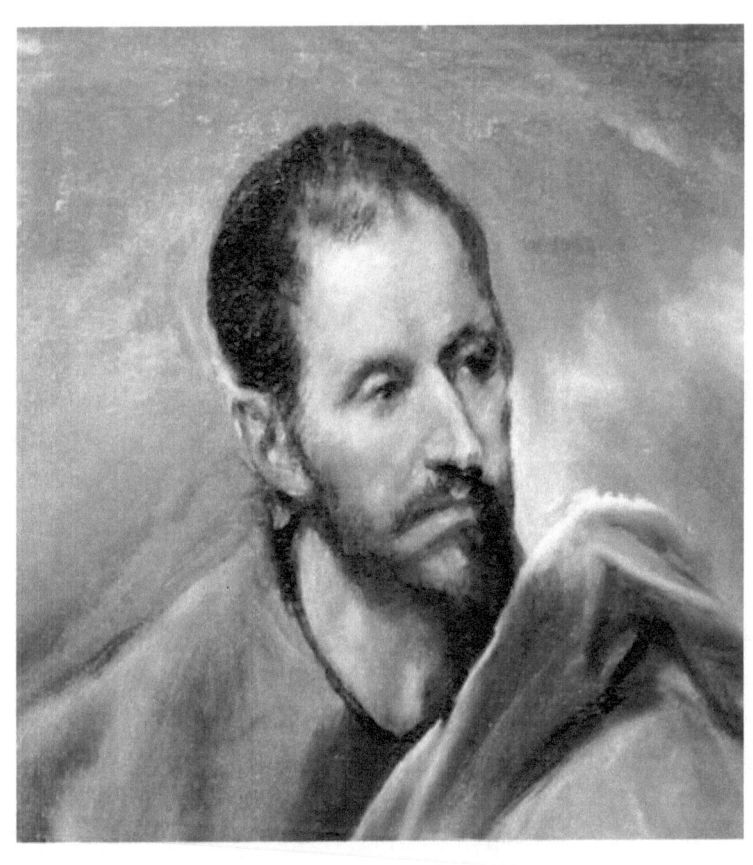

Portrait of a man, 1595, oil on canvas

Likenesses have a special place in El Greco's work. Although he was primarily interested in painting religious subjects for ecclesiastical commissions, he also produced some outstandings portraits, often inserting them into his religious compositions, as for example in the famous "Burial of Count Orgaz" in Toledo. His formal portraits and studies from life are characterized by an element of drama and a penetrating insight into the character of the sitter. He was not interested in depicting the background, nor in the insignia of rank or office which would indicate the subject's worldly status or occupation, and his sitters nearly always face the spectator and their faces reveal the soul within.

No doubt the Study of a Man is a likeness, though we do not know the identity of the model nor in what connection it came to be produced. The sketchy greenish-purplish draperies and the cloud-streaked blue background are a perfect foil for the thin ascetic face with its sparse beard. The picture was usually believed to represent El Greco himself, but as a result of recent research it is now thought to be one of a series of likenesses of the Apostles - painted from an unknown model in Toledo.

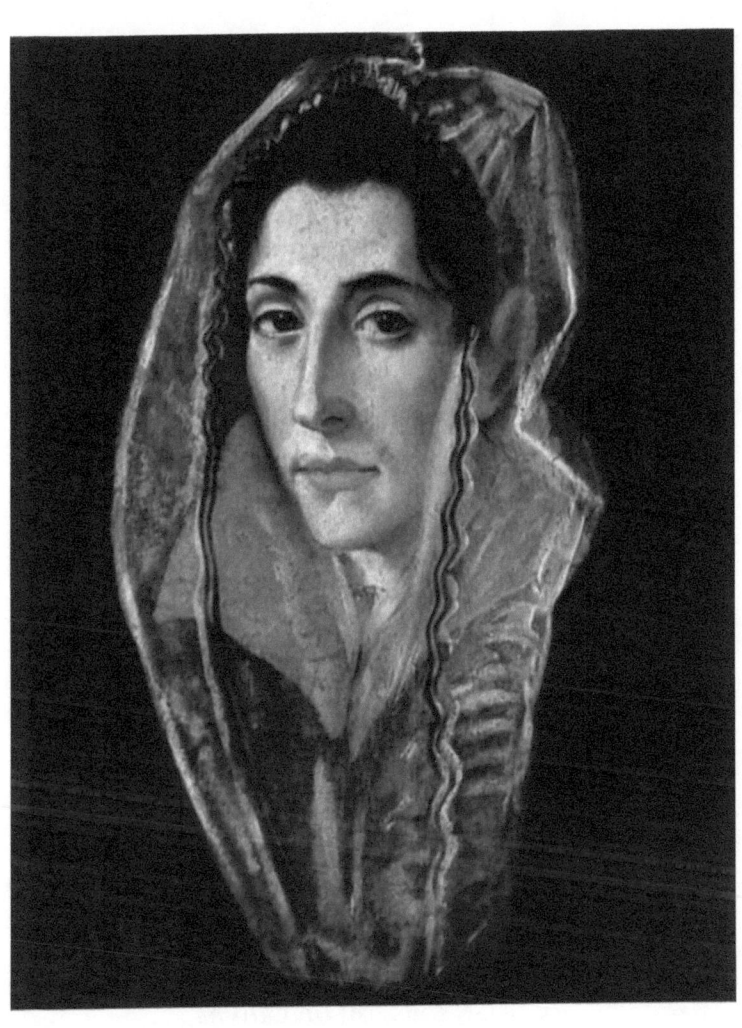

Portrait of a Lady, 1595, oil on canvas

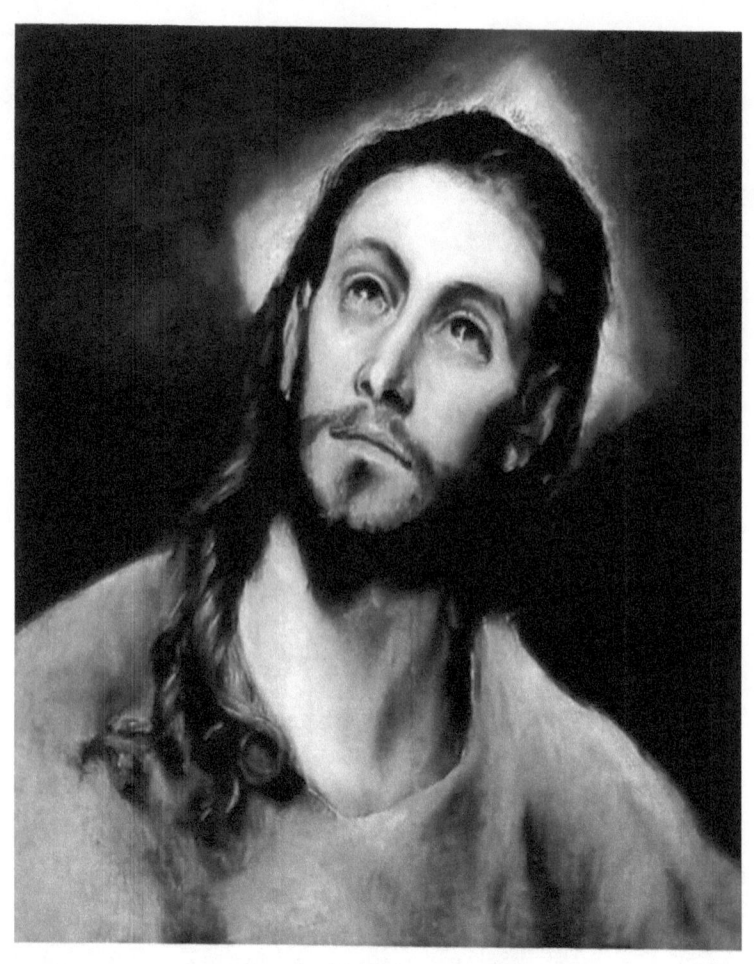

Christ, 1595, oil on canvas

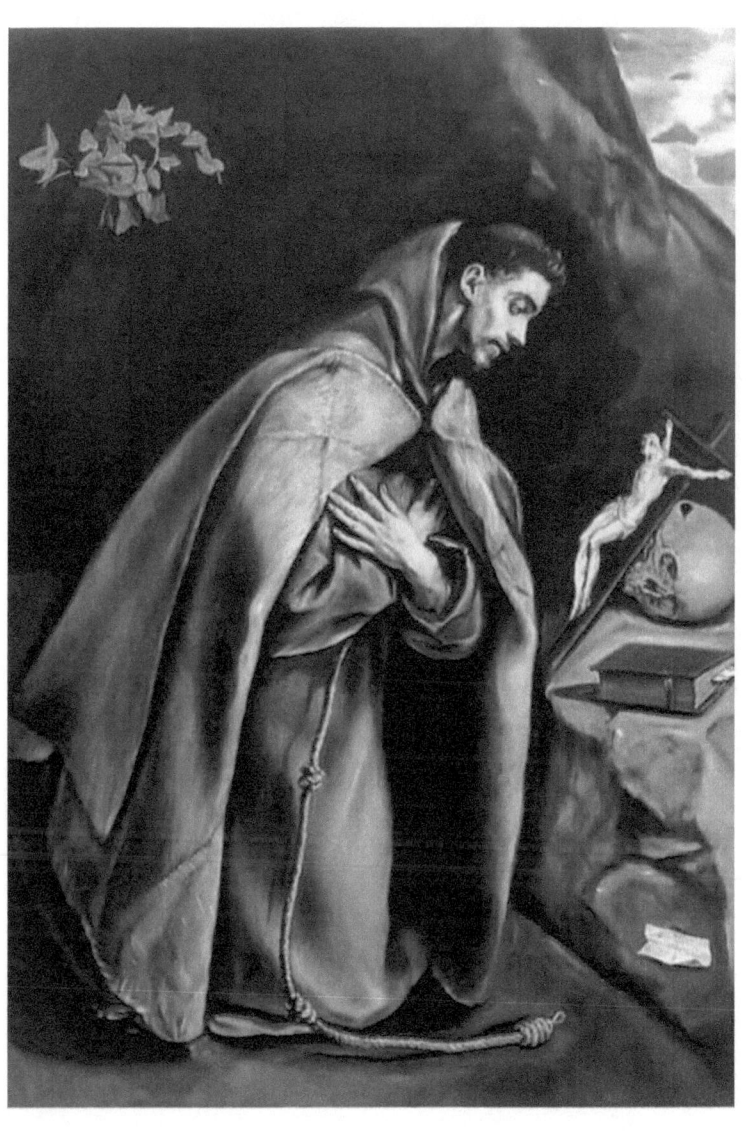

Meditation of St. Francis, 1595, oil on canvas

St Francis of Assisi was the most popular saint in the Counter-Reformation period. Favoured subjects represented in painting were his stigmatisation, his ecstasy and his meditation. El Greco treated all three, and ten different compositions by the artist can be differentiated, some half-length, some full-length, some showing the saint alone, others with a companion.

In this painting St Francis meditates not so much on mortality (signified by the skull) as on the sacrifice of Christ. In accordance with devotional practice, Francis has prepared his meditation by first reading from the Bible, shown lying on the ledge with a piece of paper marking the place.

The painting is signed on a piece of paper attached with a seal to the rock lower right.

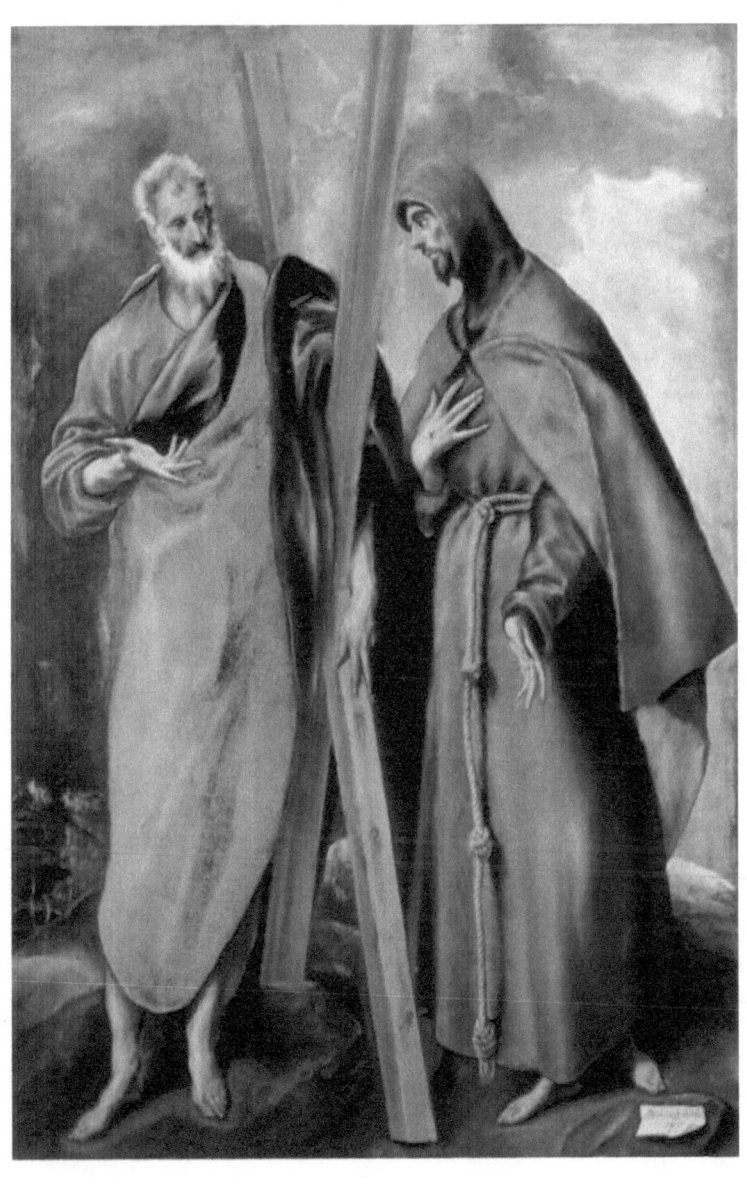

St Andrew and St Francis, 1595, Oil on canvas, 167 x 113 cm

El Greco would have been aware of the grand series of pairs of Saints painted by Navarrete for the chapels of the Church of the Escorial, the commission interrupted by the latter's death in 1579. From the time of the Burial of the Count of Orgaz, El Greco began to create his own images of the different Saints. Once a pattern was created, he kept closely to it.

The pairing of Saints - the juxtaposition of two separate personalities, with their different spiritual significance - accentuates the individual characters. Saint Peter and Saint Paul, the two Saint Johns, were more obvious juxtapositions, but he also brought together such unlikely characters as in the present painting - the one, the somewhat austere Apostle and Martyr of the time of Christ; the other, the ecstatic and 'gentle' Saint of the Middle Ages. The landscape also is double. The Saint Francis derives from the figure on the left of the Burial of the Count of Orgaz, and has become more spiritualised; the Saint Andrew is the same type as that of the Talavera painting of 1591, and the gesture is a remarkable development of the similar gesture of the Saint Maurice, in the Escorial painting, and eventually, indeed, can be traced back to the early Healing of the Blind.

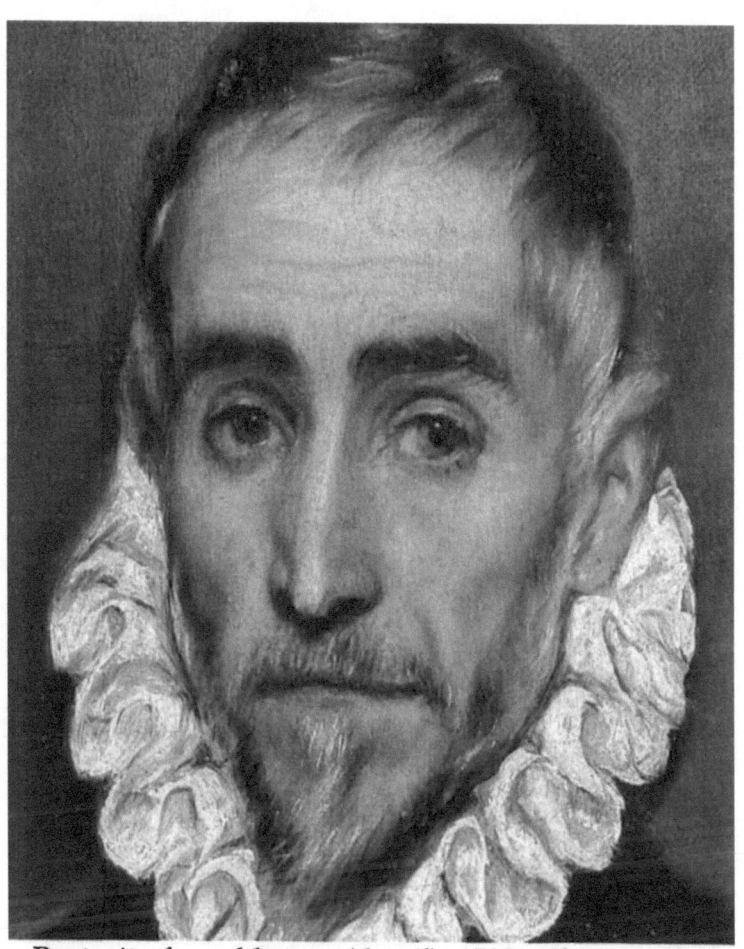

Portrait of a nobleman (detail), 1595, oil on canvas

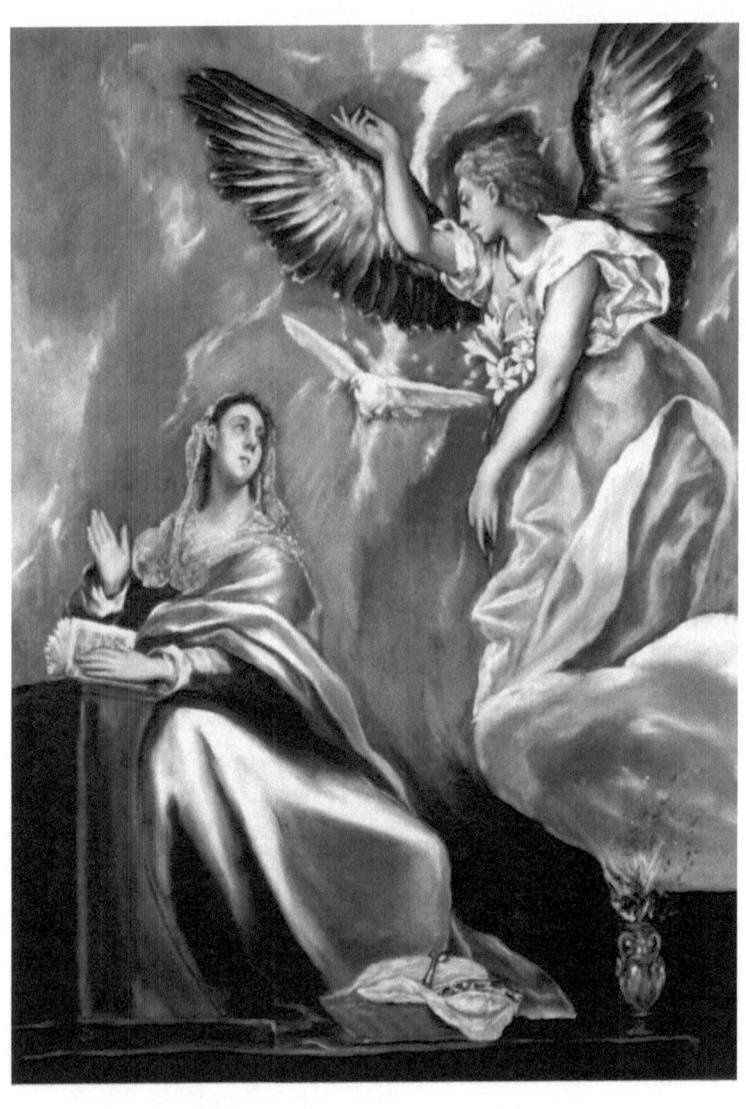

Annunciation, 1595-1600, Oil on canvas, 91 x 66, 5 cm

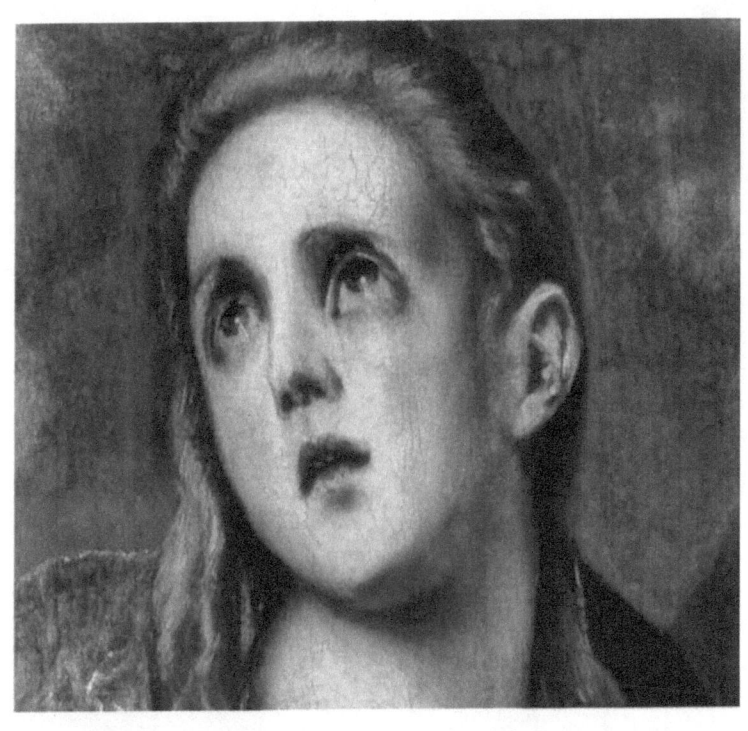

Penitence of Magdalene (detail), 1597, oil on canvas

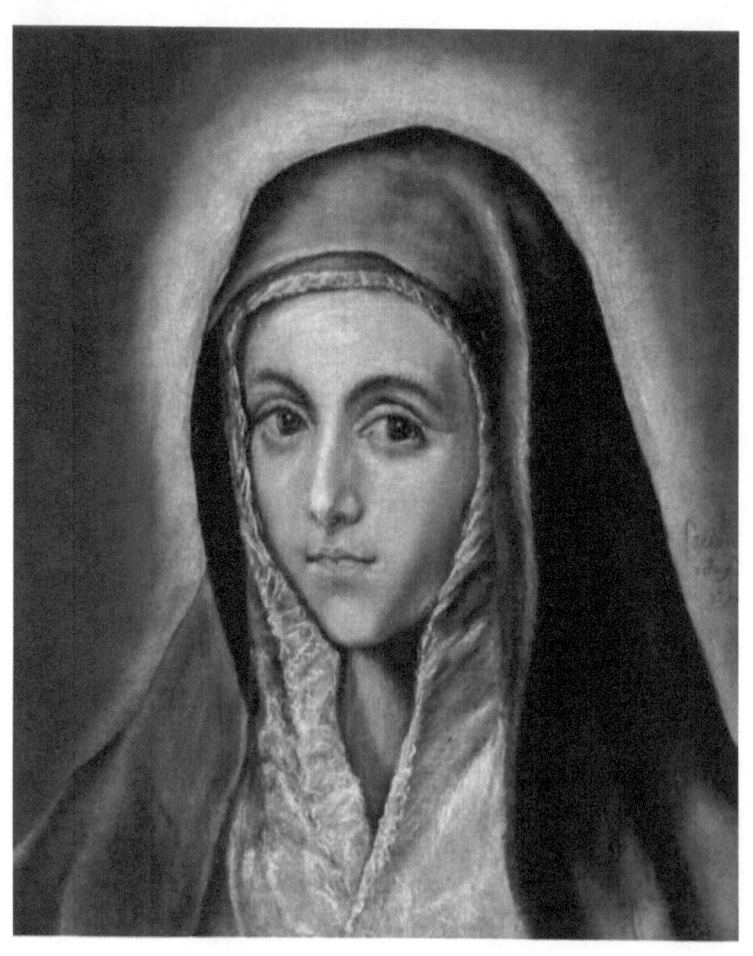

Virgin 1597, oil on canvas

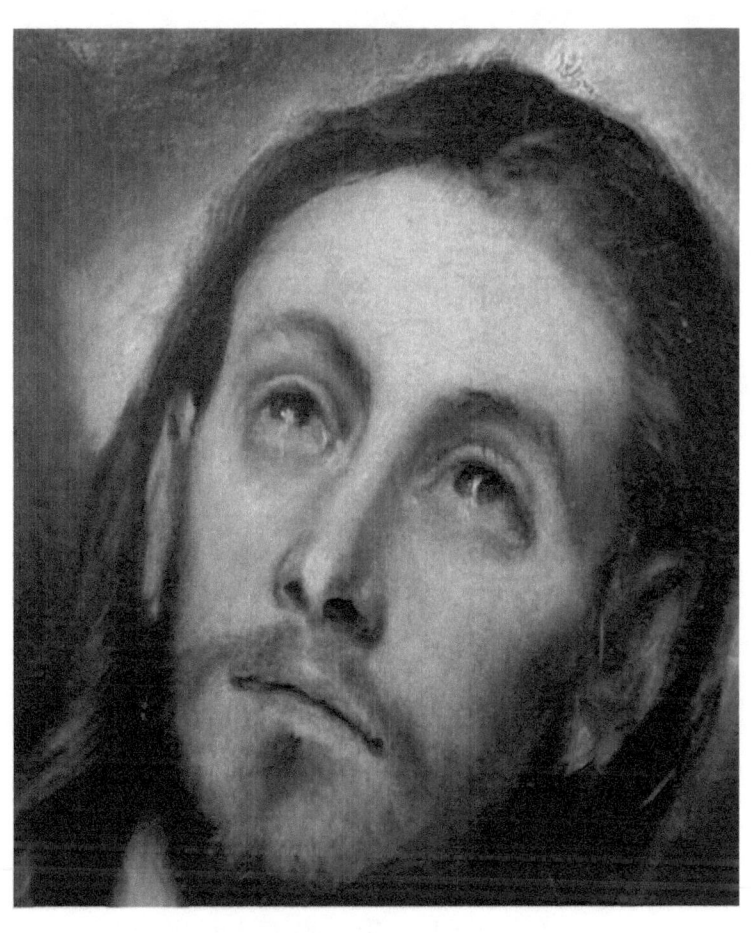

Praying Christ (detail), 1597, oil on canvas

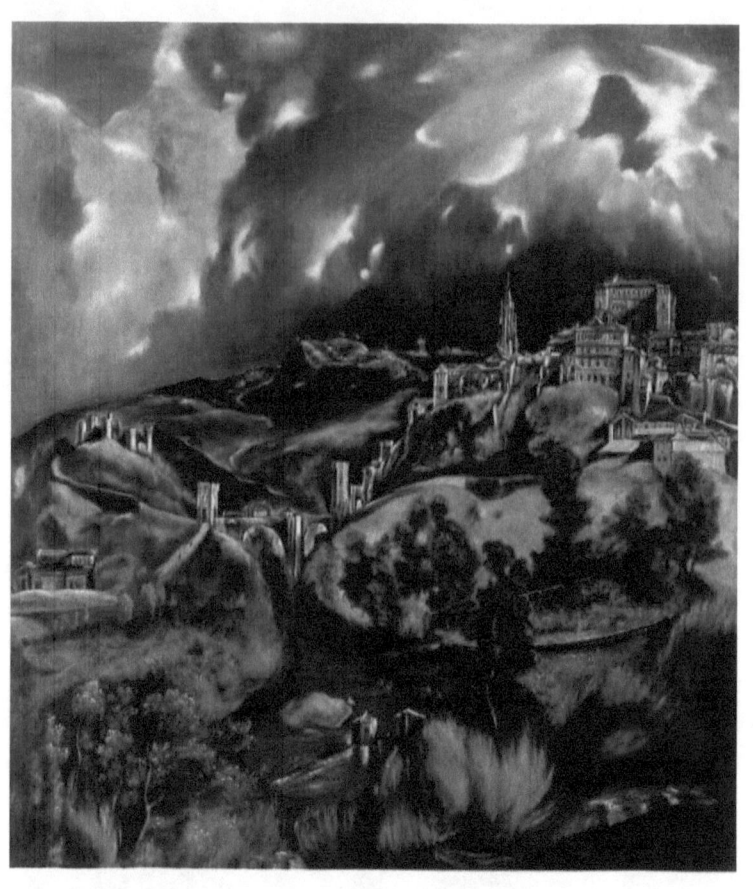

A View of Toledo, 1597-99, Oil on canvas

There are two surviving landscapes by El Greco: The View of Toledo (Metropolitan Museum, New York) and the View and Plan of Toledo (Museo de El Greco, Toledo). They respond to very different objectives: one setting out to document the city in cartographic terms, the other evoking it through a selective arrangement of its most characteristic features. The Metropolitan painting belongs to a tradition of emblematic city views; its approach is interpretative rather than documentary: it seeks to portray the essence of the city rather than to record its actual appearance.

Both in here and in the View and Plan the city is shown from the north, except that El Greco has included only the easternmost portion, above the Tagus river. This partial view would have excluded the cathedral, which he therefore imaginatively moved to the left of the dominant Alcőzar or royal palace. The fact that an identical view appears in the Saint Joseph and the Christ Child in the Capilla de San Josŭ suggests that the painting was conceived in connection with the San Josŭ commission (1597-99). From that time, the town features in many of his paintings: in the Laocoɪn (National Gallery of Art, Washington), the Christ in Agony on the Cross (Cincinnati Art Museum), the Virgin of the Immaculate Conception (Museo de Santa Cruz), in all of which it takes on an apocalyptical character appropriate to the themes. In his late Saint John the Baptist (Fine Arts Museums of San Francisco) the landscape of the Escorial is appropriately introduced.

This is one of the earliest independent landscapes in Western art and one of the most dramatic and individual landscapes ever painted. It is not just a 'View of Toledo', although the topographical details are correct; neither is it 'Toledo at night' or 'Toledo in a storm', other titles which have been attached to the painting: it is simply 'Toledo', but Toledo given a universal meaning - a spiritual portrait of the town. In introducing the view into his paintings he acknowledges how much his art owed to the inspiration of the town, until a few years before the great Imperial Capital and still the great ecclesiastical and cultural centre of Spain - the town isolated on the plain of Castile which he had made his new home, so far from the island of his birth.

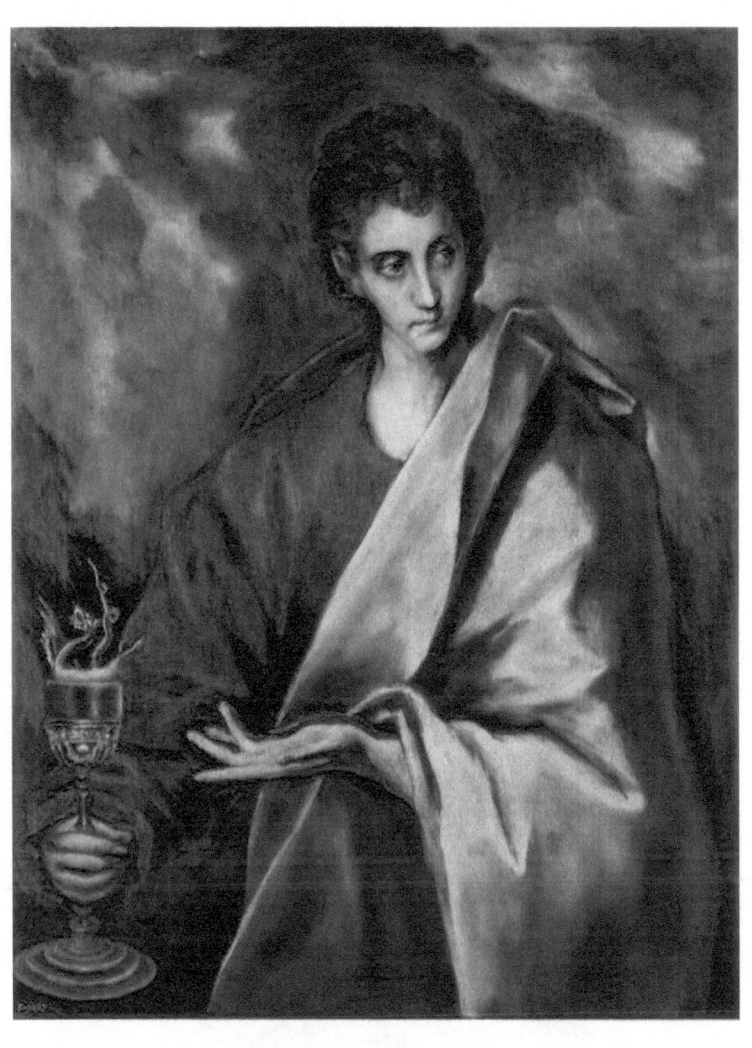

St John the Evangelist, 1595-1604, Oil on canvas, 90 x 77 cm

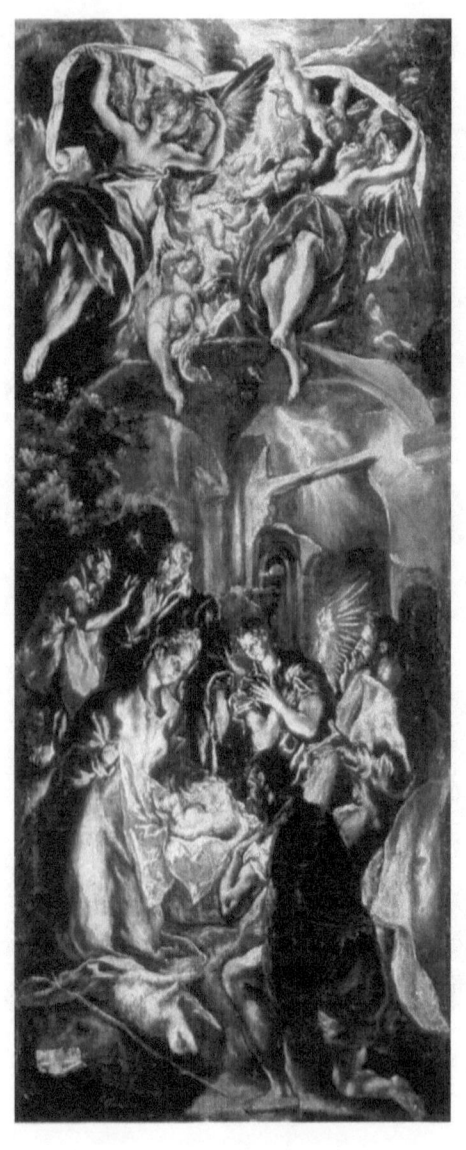

Adoration of the Shepherds, 1596-1600, Oil on canvas,
11 x 47 cm

The two paintings in the Galleria Nazionale d'Arte Antica in Rome (Adoration of the Shepherds, Baptism of Christ) were considered workshop pieces or autograph replicas of two of the three pictures that El Greco executed for the Colegio di Doña Marнa de Aragyn in Madrid (now dispersed and housed in the Muzeul de Arta, Bucharest and the Museo del Prado, Madrid). However, a recent radiographic analysis (1997) has proven that they are original oil sketches by the hand of El Greco himself. The presence of pentimenti, compositional emendations beneath the paint surface, reveals the creative process of the artist and leads to the conclusion that these are not copies but preparatory bozzetti for the Madrid cycle. The important commission, probably designed as a triptych to decorate the high altar of the chapel, was given to El Greco in 1596: work continued until the Holy Year of 1600. The third oil sketch, depicting the Annunciation, is preserved at the museum in Bilbao. The silvery light, the coloristic range based on cold tones, the quick, almost impressionistic brushwork and the use of strong contrasts of light and shadow in this picture are all typical characteristics of El Greco's Spanish manner (1576-1614).

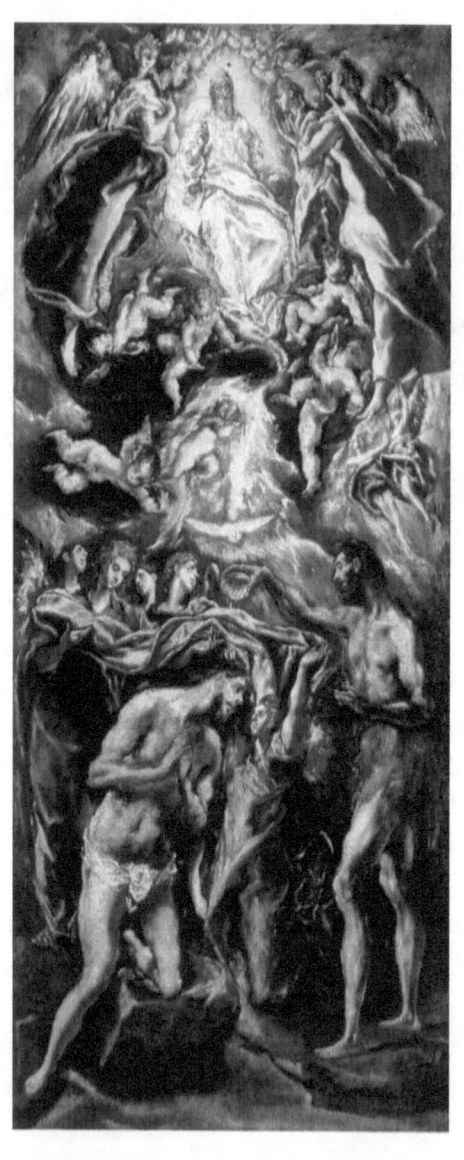

Baptism of Christ, 1596-1600, Oil on canvas, 111 x 47 cm

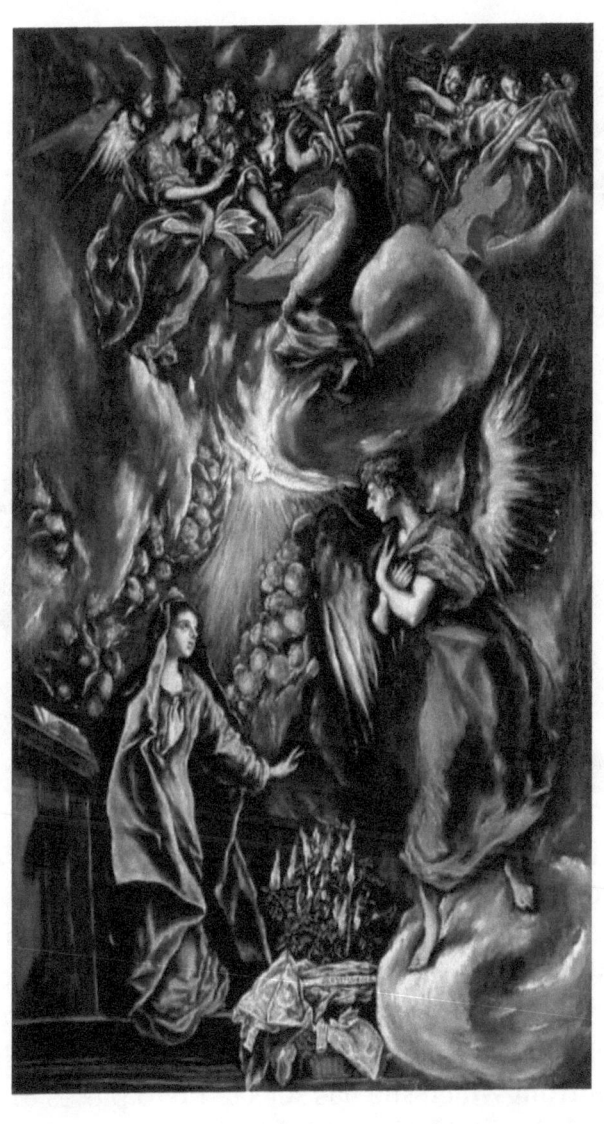

The Annunciation, 1596-1600, Oil on canvas, 113,5 x 66 cm

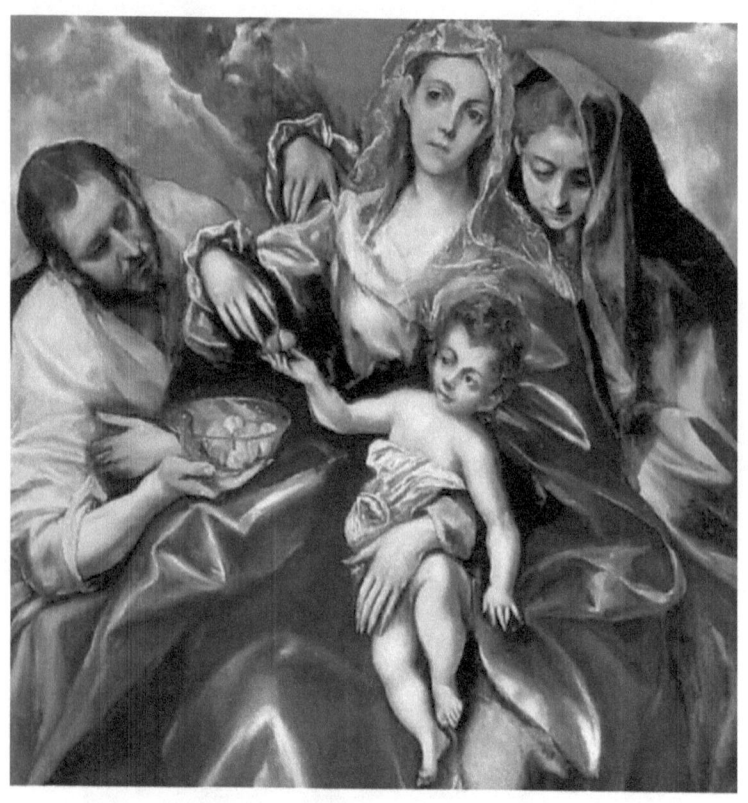

Holy Family with Mary Magdalene, 1598, oil on canvas
This composition of the Holy Family with St Mary
Magdalen was repeated many times by El Greco's
workshop and imitators. In the painting, pervaded by a
warm domesticity, we can find an anecdotal approach
to a religious theme: St Joseph offers the Virgin a bowl
of fruit from which she has selected two pieces to give
to the Christ Child. This still-life detail of the clear glass
bowl with fruit is the most striking feature of the
picture. It is supposed that the head of Mary is a
portrait of Doña Jerynima de las Cuevas while that of St
Joseph is a self-portrait of the artist.

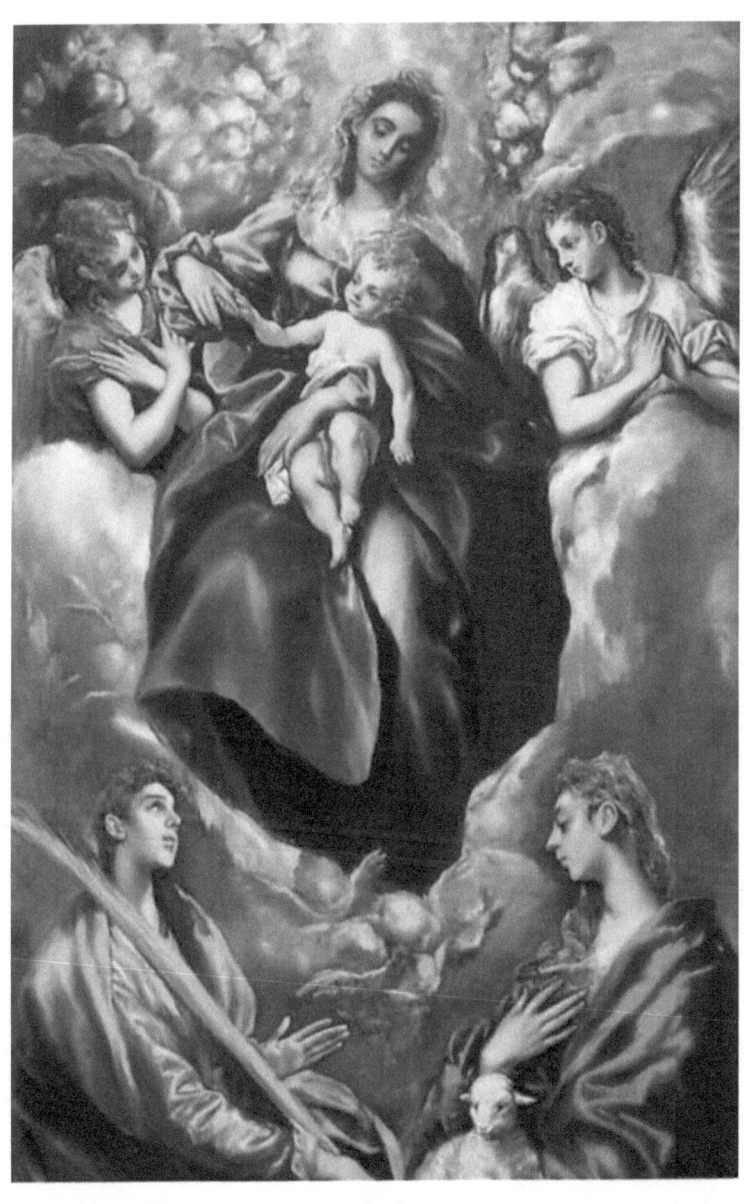

Virgin and Child with St. Martina and St. Agnes, 1599,
oil on canvas

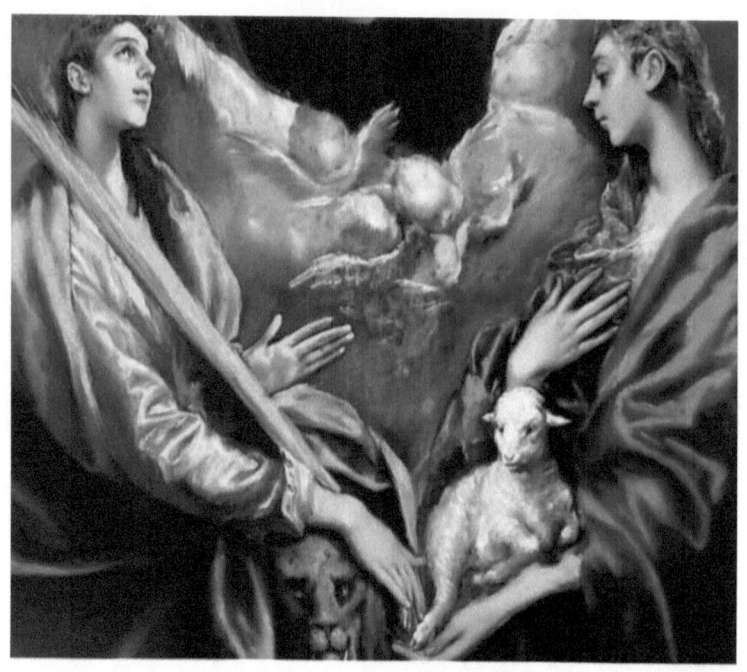

Virgin and Child with St. Martina and St. Agnes, detail,
1599, oil on canvas

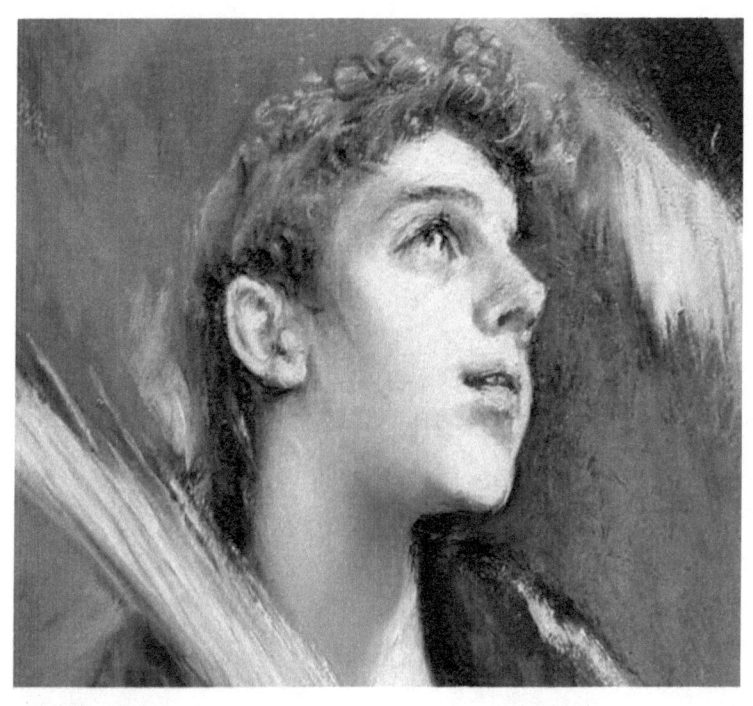

Virgin and Child with St Martina and St Agnes (detail), 1599, oil on canvas

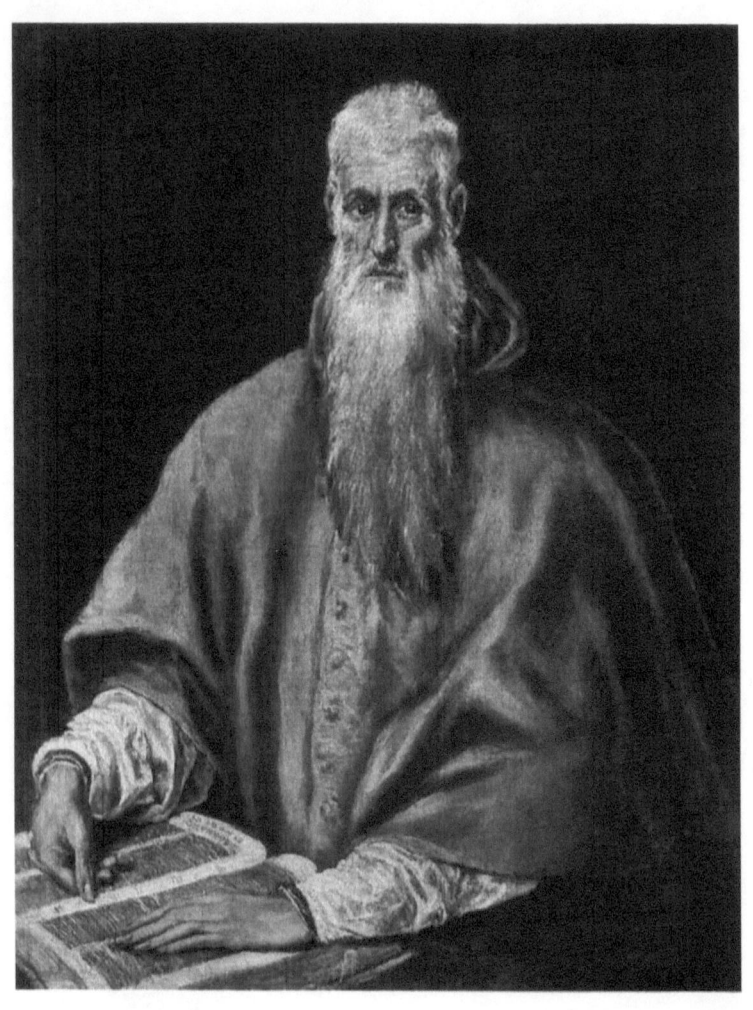

St Jerome as Cardinal, c. 1600, Oil on canvas, 59 x 48 cm

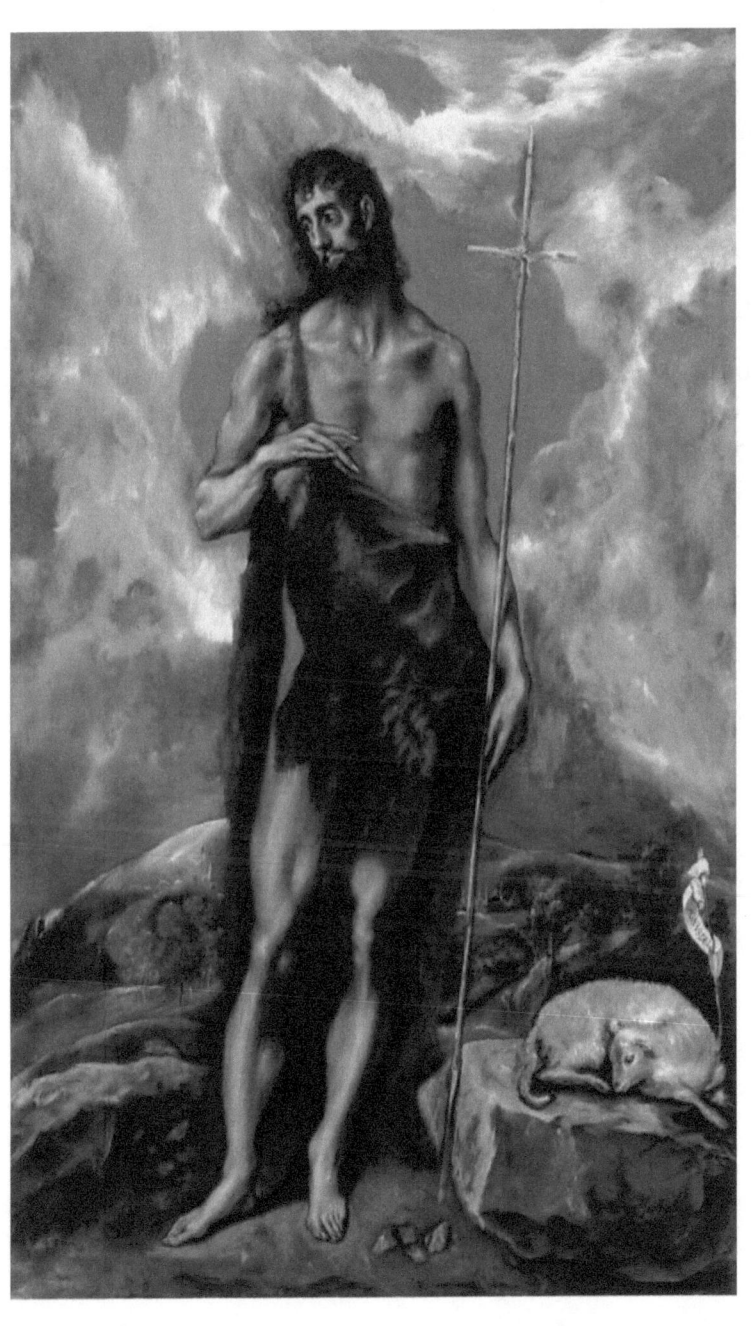

St. John the Baptist, c. 1600, Oil on canvas, 111 x 66 cm

This is the finest of the various representations in which this figure of St John the Baptist appears. The attenuated figure, the agitated movement of the sky and the scintillating light on the landscape is characteristic of El Greco's work around 1600. This painting is distinguished from related pictures by the placement of the lamb on the rock - a reference to Christ's sacrifice. The building in the landscape background was identifies as the Escorial. A similar representation of St John the Baptist is in another painting in the Church of the Jesuits in Toledo, depicting St John the Evangelist and St John the Baptist together.

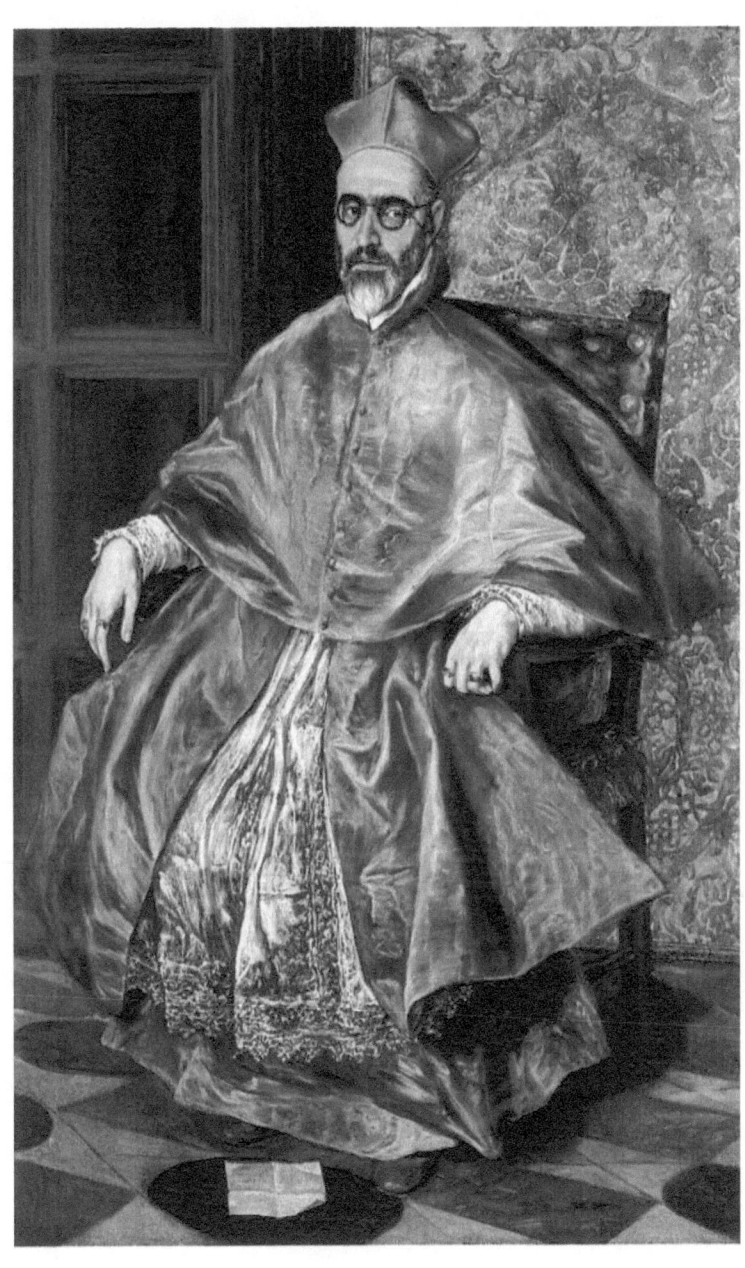

Portrait of a Cardinal, 1600, oil on canvas

The sitter is usually identified as Cardinal Don Fernando Niño de Guevera (1541-1609), Grand Inquisitor and, from 1601, Archbishop of Seville. The painting was executed c. 1600, when Inquisitor-General, and certainly before he became Archbishop of Seville. He is one of a number of eminent ecclesiastics of Toledo portrayed by El Greco, and it is one of his finest portraits. The splendour and richness of colour is appropriate to the character and rank of the sitter. The frontal turn of the pose concentrates attention on the figure. El Greco suggests the cardinal's personality through the emphasis on his prominent glasses, the compulsive gesture of his left hand, the animated, nervous brushwork, and the singular colour range. The painting is signed on the creased paper on the floor. This celebrated picture - a landmark in the history of European portraiture - has become synonymous not only with El Greco but with Spain and the Spanish Inquisition.

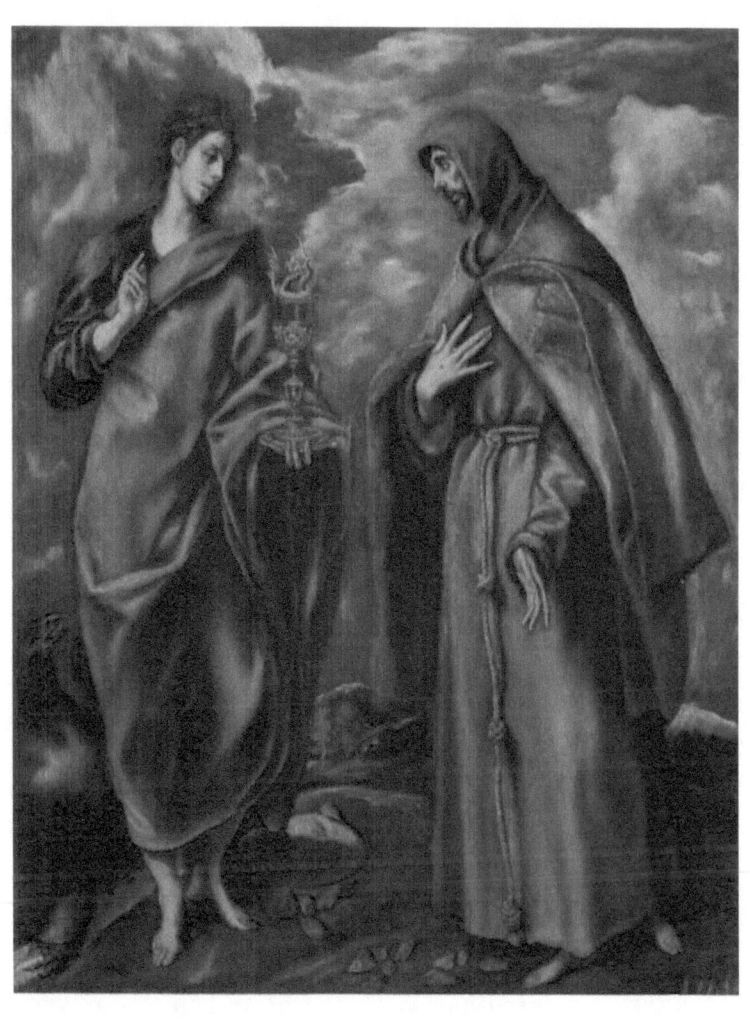

Sts John and Francis, c. 1600, Oil on canvas, 110 x 86 cm

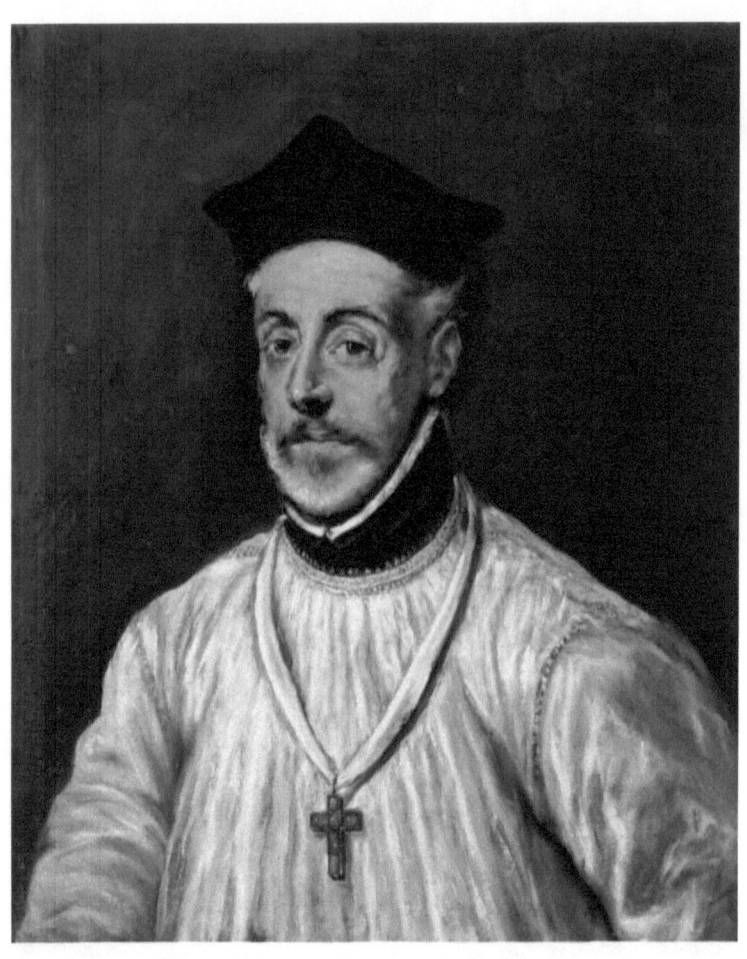

Diego de Covarrubias, c. 1600, Oil on canvas, 67 x 55 cm

Diego de Covarrubias y Leiva (1512-1577) was the elder brother of Antonio de Covarrubias, a close friend of El Greco and reputedly one of the most learned men of his time. Diego was a distinguished churchman, canon lawyer and administrator. El Greco never met him, and despite its lively character the painting was based on a portrait by Alonso Sónchez Coello showing Covarrubias when sixty-two years old. The painting has a pendant, also in the Museo de El Greco, showing Diego's younger brother Antonio - an autograph copy of El Greco's painting in the Louvre.

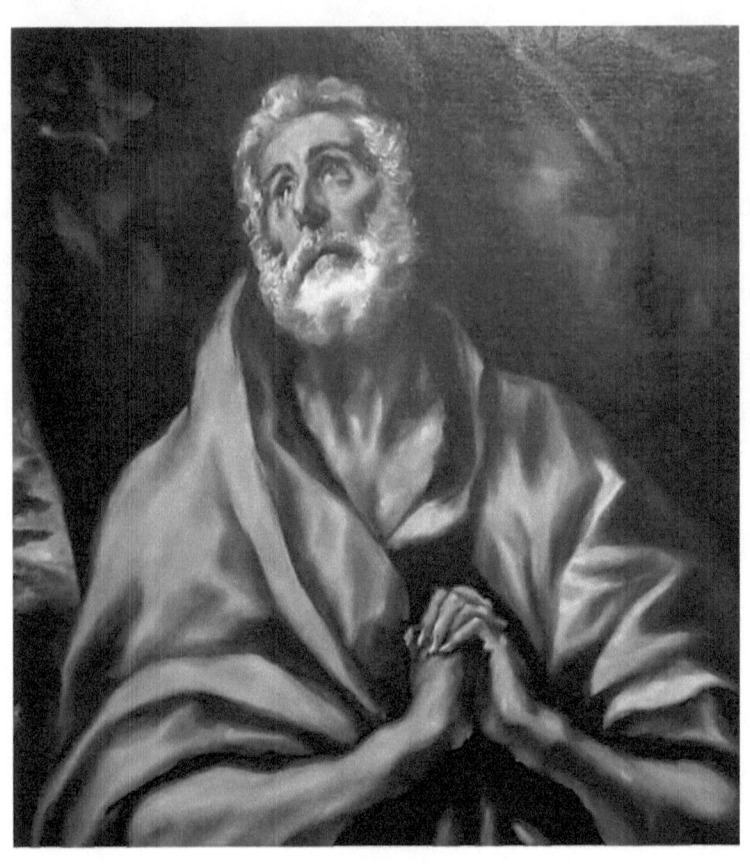

The penitent St. Peter, 1600, oil on canvas

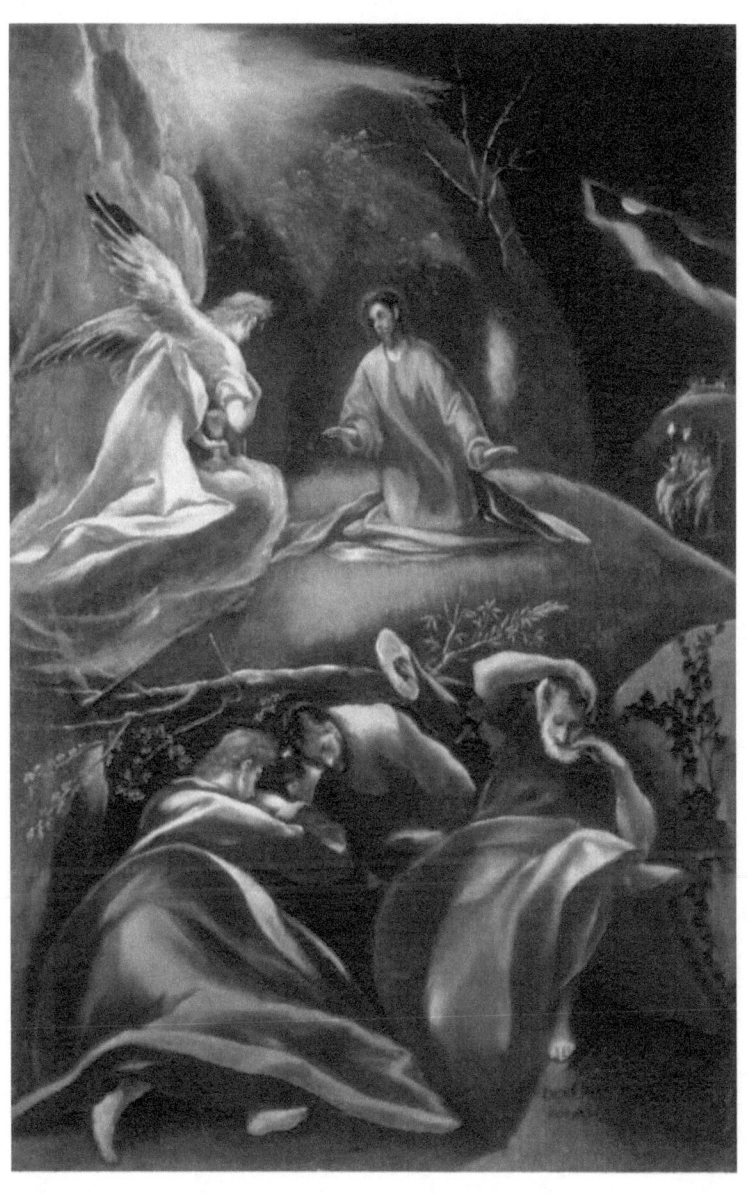

The Agony in the Garden, 1600-05, Oil on canvas, 169 x 112 cm

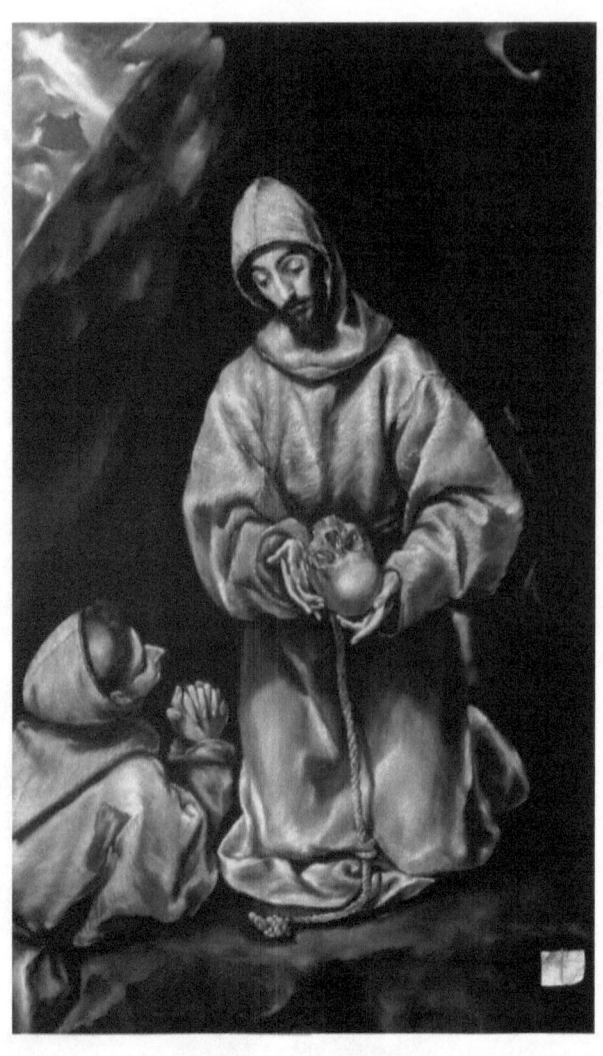

St Francis and Brother Leo Meditating on Death, 1600-02, Oil on canvas, 168,5 x 103,2 cm

El Greco's representations of St Francis were highly popular in Spain. El Greco no longer depicted the saint, as was previously common, at the moment of his stigmatization, that is, his miraculous reception of Christ's wounds, but in the process of musing over a skull. The founder of the Jesuit order, Ignatius of Loyola, had recommended the use of a skull in meditational practices in his Spiritual Exercises.

No one had captured the figure of the order's founder as described in the chronicles like El Greco, about forty versions of whose composition are still in existence even today. Two other factors probably also contributed to its extraordinary success: first, the great veneration enjoyed by St Francis in Spain - in Toledo alone, there were ten Franciscan religious institutions - and second, the recourse to modern media of dissemination.

This painting is one of the many representations of St Francis by El Greco in which the saint is shown with Brother Leo, his faithful companion, at the entrance to a cave on Mount Alverna, where towards the end of his life St Francis retired for fasting and prayer. There exist some forty versions of this successful composition, consisting of autograph works, workshop paintings, early variants and copies. Because El Greco knew from Italy how important reproduction prints were in popularizing new visual ideas, he had an engraving done of his work in 1606 under his supervision by his pupil Diego de Astor.

This version is an autograph work, it was intended for personal devotion, and El Greco has placed the skull virtually in the centre of the composition, and frontally, so that it acts as the focus for the viewer's meditation.

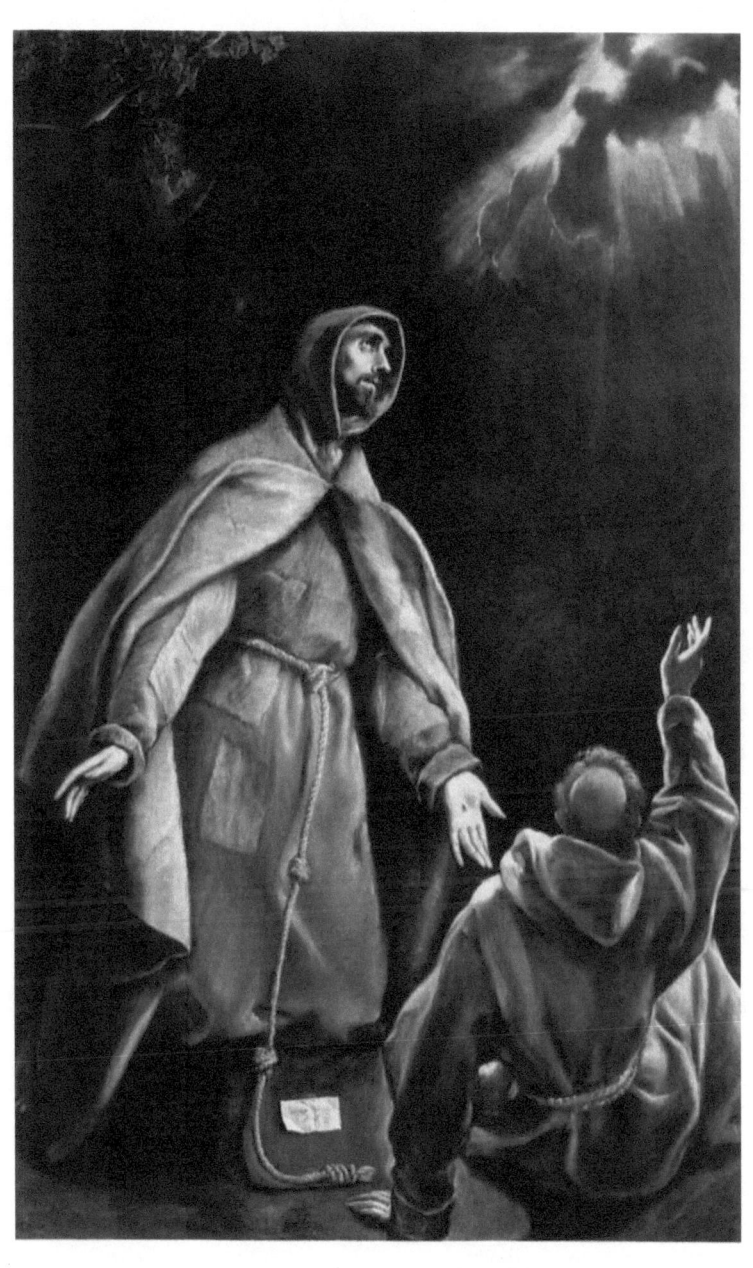

St Francis's Vision of the Flaming Torch, 1600-05, Oil on
canvas, 203 x 148 cm

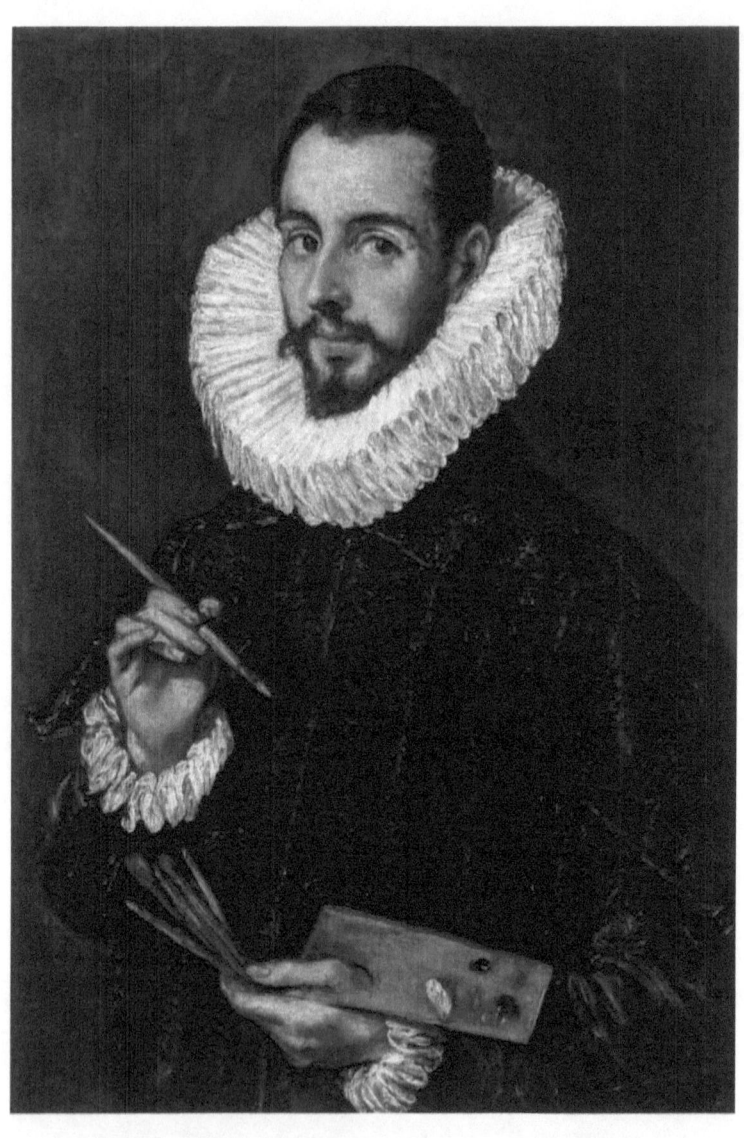

Portrait of the Artist's Son Jorge Manuel
Theotokopoulos, c. 1603, Oil on canvas, 74 x 51,5 cm

Long thought to be a self-portrait by El Greco, this painting is now universally agreed to represent the painter's son, Jorge Manuel Theotokopoulos (1578-1631). Jorge Manuel appears about the same age as in the Virgin of Charity, painted 1603-05, that is, when he was twenty-five to twenty-seven years old. The young gentleman, of a certain aristocratic mien, displays elegantly the tools of his craft. It is one of his most splendid portraits, but it is with difficulty that one relates the personality to that of the Saint Luke. Jorge Manuel was not a remarkable painter like his father. Here El Greco depicts his son as an artist and at the same time as a member of the upper class.

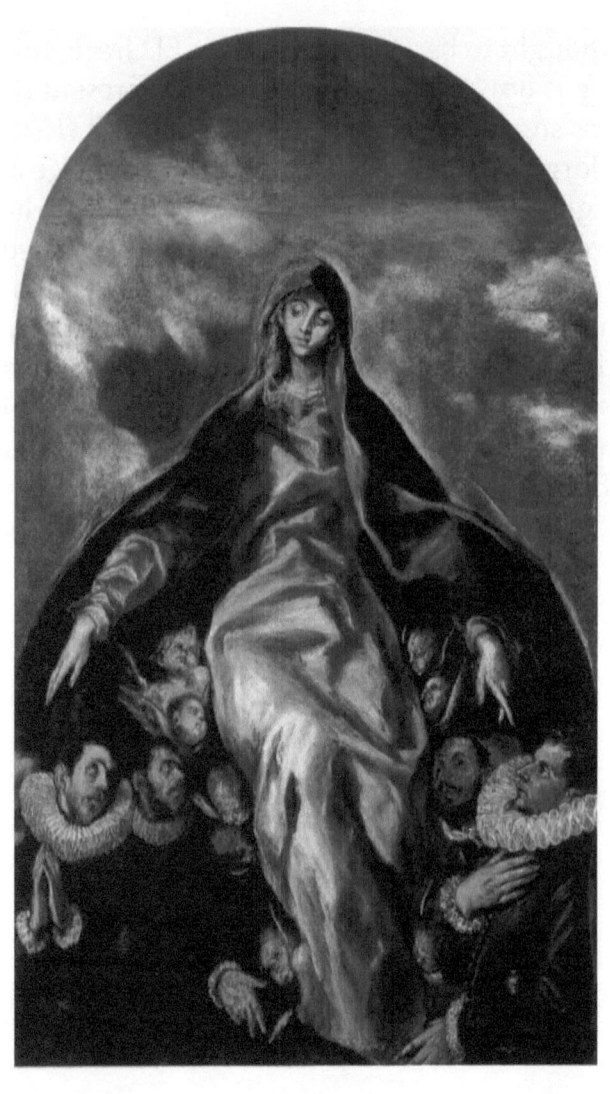

The Madonna of Charity, 1603-05, Oil on canvas, 155 x
123 cm

On 18 June 1603 El Greco signed a contract to make and decorate an altarpiece for a miraculous image of the Virgin of Charity belonging to the Hospital de la Caridad in the small town of Illescas halfway between Toledo and Madrid. According to the contract the main altarpiece and the decoration of the vault were to contain four canvases: The Madonna of Charity, The Coronation of the Virgin, The Annunciation and The Nativity. This project was executed in collaboration with the artist's son, Jorge Manual Theotokopoulos. Under a separate contract a further painting, St Ildefonso was made.

All the portraits The Madonna of Charity are of men of Toledo of El Greco's time. The ruffs had grown to rather exaggerated proportions in the twenty years from the time of the Burial of the Count of Orgaz, and their introduction into the painting was censured by the Hospital authorities. At some time they were painted over, but have been recently restored. El Greco's son appears on the extreme right, at about the same age as in the portrait in Seville.

Presently the painting is located in a side altar balancing the painting of St Ildefonso.

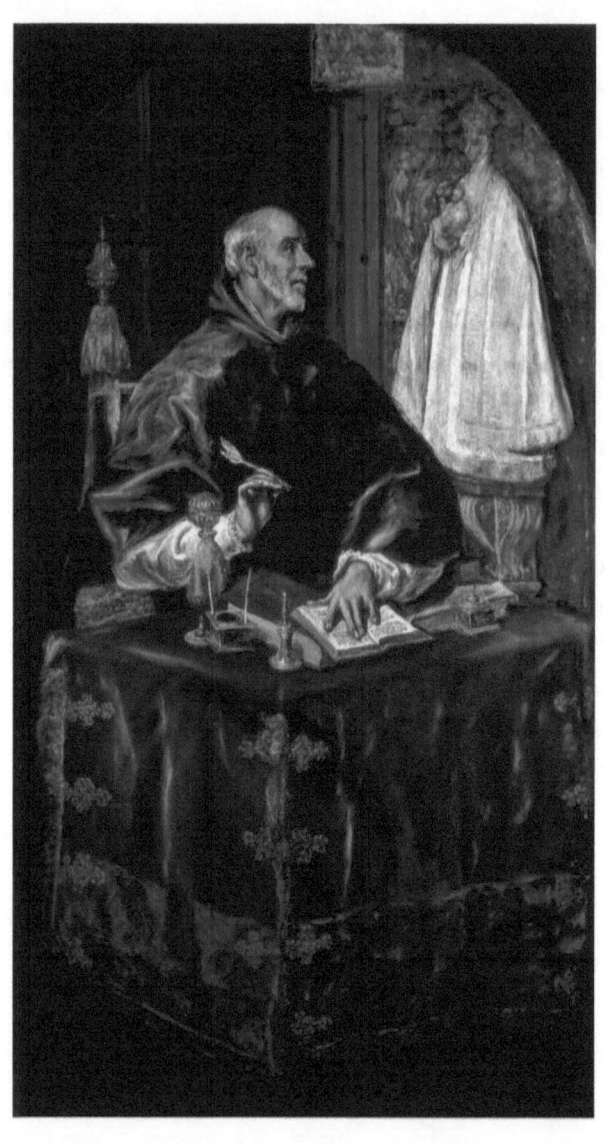

St Ildefonso, 1603-05, Oil on canvas, 187 x 102 cm

In collaboration with his son Jorge Manuel in 1603-07, El Greco executed an extensive programme of pictures for the Hospital de la Caridad in Illescas: a Madonna of Charity, a Coronation of the Virgin, an Annunciation, and a Nativity. Under a separate contract a further picture was made, of St Ildefonso, who was particularly important for Toledo.

The painting is in the side altar on the left of the main chapel of the church, balancing the Virgin of Charity. Its original place in the church is not known. The painting is not mentioned in the incomplete documentation for the decoration of the chapel, and if, as is probable, it was not painted at the same time, it cannot date much before June 1603, the date of the contract, and was more likely painted soon after the conclusion of litigation in August 1607. In its present position, it makes a grand pair to the Virgin of Charity, and is one of the most splendid of his 'portraits' of Saints.

It is difficult, and perhaps not proper, to separate his portraits of Saints from his actual portraits. In both he employs all his means of spiritual or psychological expression. The legend is that Saint Ildefonso, the first Bishop of Toledo, presented an image of the Virgin of the Mantle to a foundation of his in Illescas. The Saint is portrayed before the same image, as he wrote his dissertation on the Purity of the Virgin. The state of inspiration is brilliantly expressed. There is an infinite distinction in expression between the hand poised with the pen in this 'portrait' and the similar motif in the portrait of his son.

In his depiction of St Ildefonso, El Greco anticipated a Baroque motif, that of the learned churchman. As if receiving inspiration, the saint is seated at a desk covered with an array of utensils that is unusually detailed for the artist.

There is a smaller replica of the picture in the National Gallery of Art in Washington. It belonged once to the painter Jean Fran3ois Millet, and later to Edgar Degas.

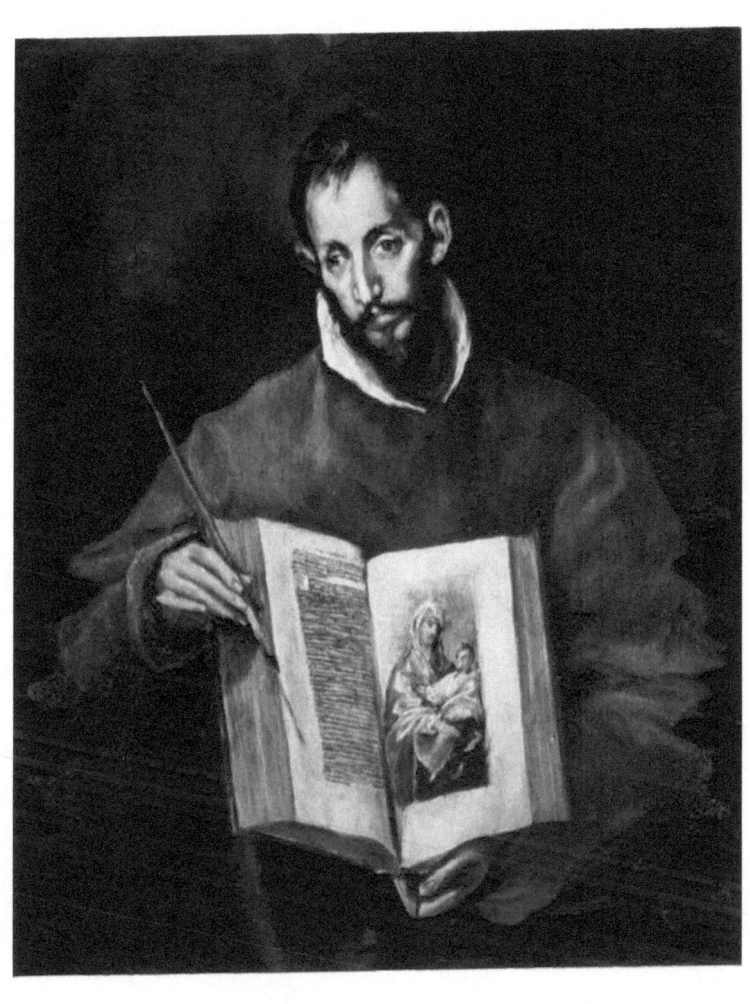

St Luke, 1605-10, Oil on canvas, 98 x 72 cm

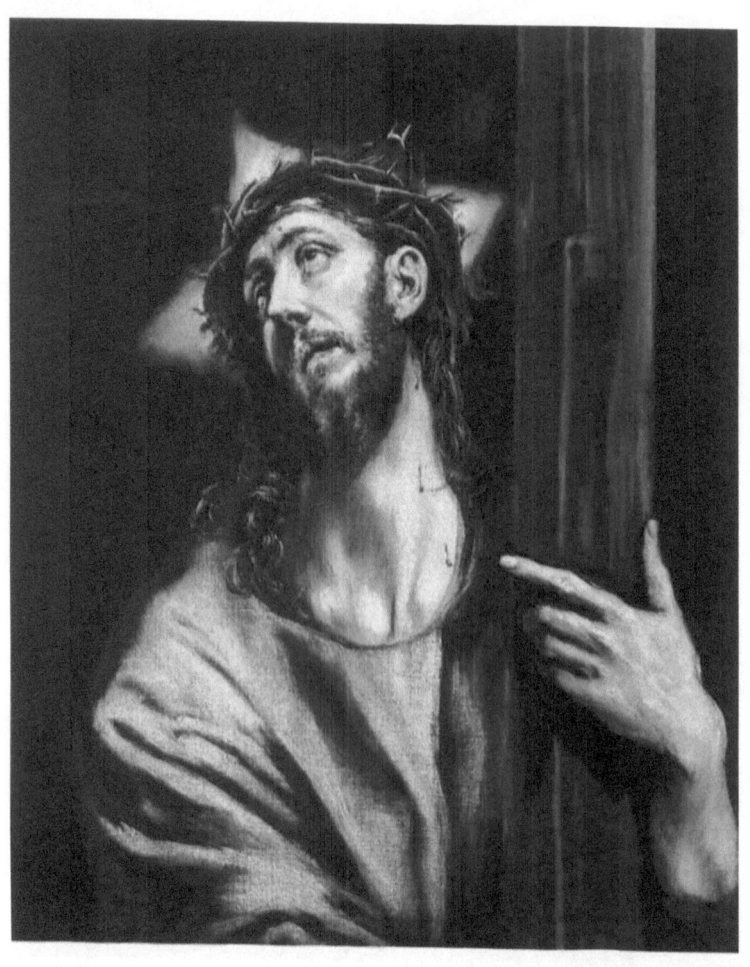

Christ Holding the Cross, 1602-07, Oil on canvas, 66 x 53 cm

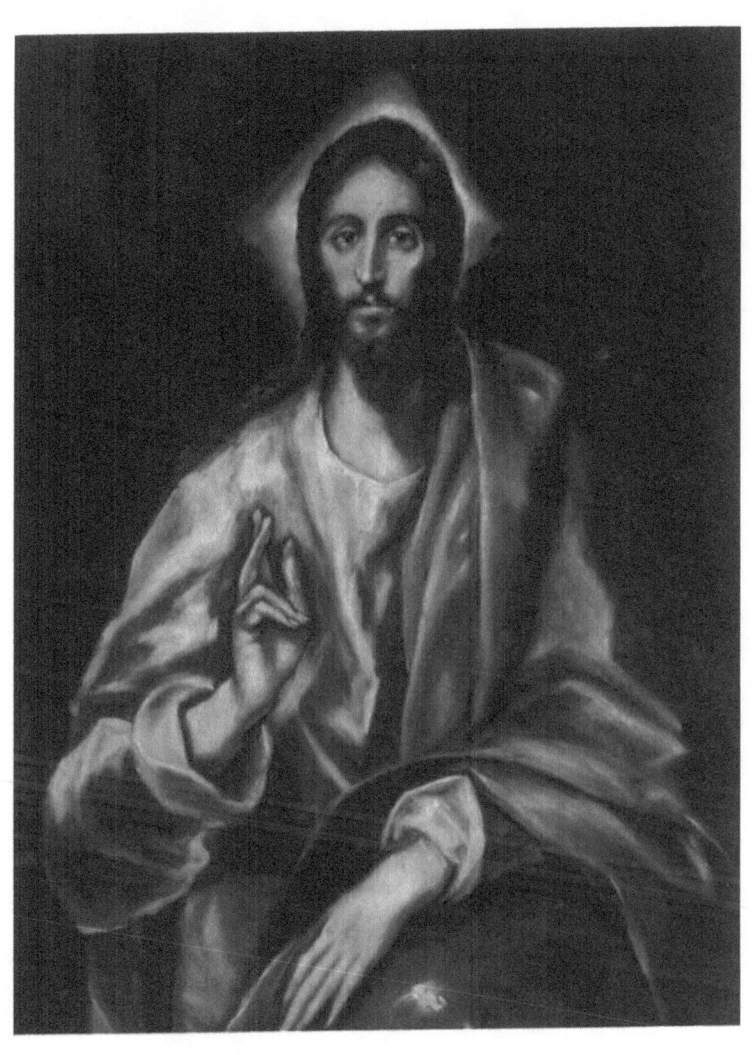

Christ, c. 1606, Oil on canvas, 98 x 78 cm

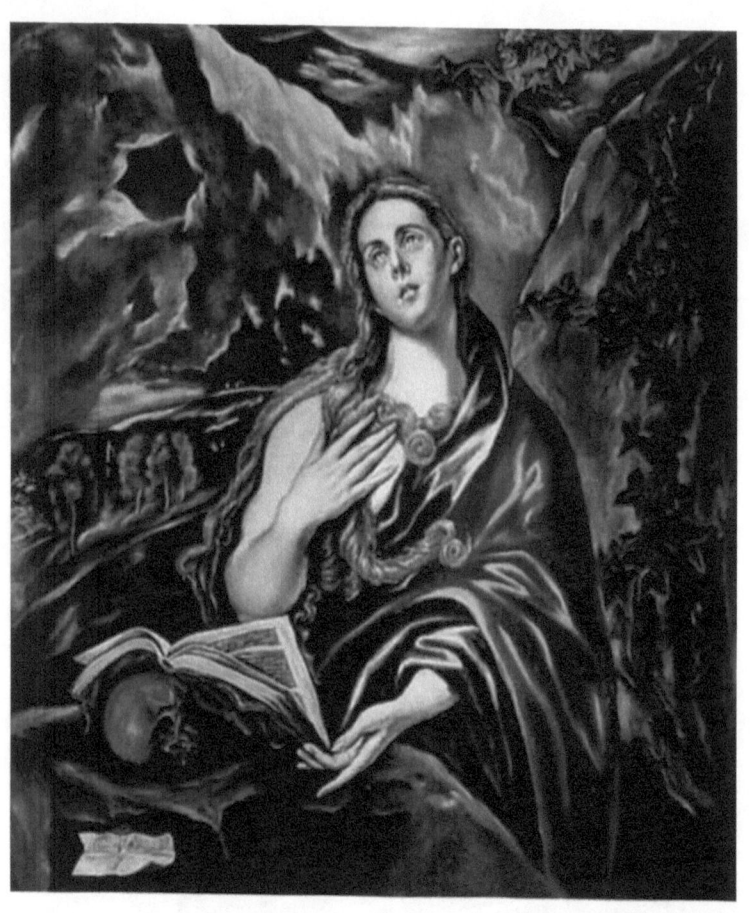

Penitent Magdalen, 1605-10, Oil on canvas, 118 x 105
cm

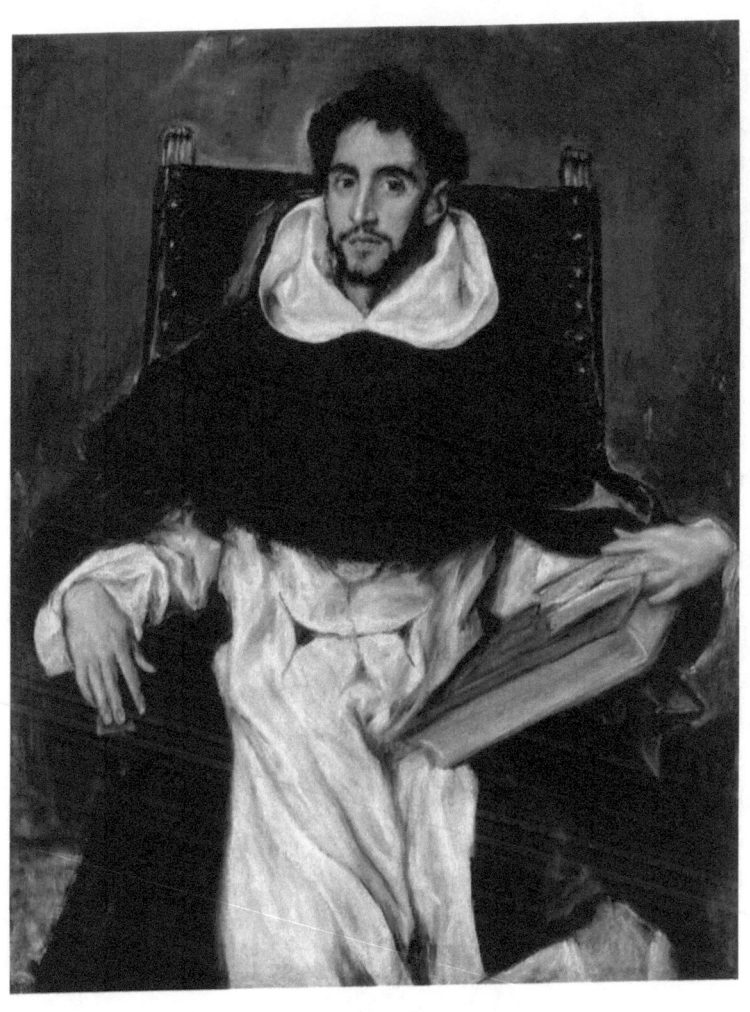

Fray Hortensio Felix Paravicino, c. 1609, Oil on canvas,
112 x 86 cm

Hortensio Felix Paravicino y Arteaga (1580-1633) was a Trinitarian friar who came to know El Greco during the painter's last years. His family was of Italian origin but he was born in Madrid. Already Professor of Rhetoric at the University of Salamanca at the age of twenty-one, he was a figure of great intellectual brilliance and authority in the Spain of Philip III and Philip IV. He was a prolific poet and renowned orator. Paravicino dedicated four sonnets to El Greco's memory in a volume of poems published in 1641. This included the oft-quoted lines: 'Crete gave him life, Toledo his brushes and a better homeland...' Another of the sonnets, celebrating the portrait, tells us that it was painted when poet was twenty-nine years of age.

The complete frontality of the pose, the enormous simplicity, and the absence of any setting contribute to the feeling of spiritual presence, comparatively absent from the splendid portrait of Cardinal Guevara. The inspired rhythm and handling is no less a living thing than the man himself. It is one of the greatest masterpieces of portraiture and painting of all time.

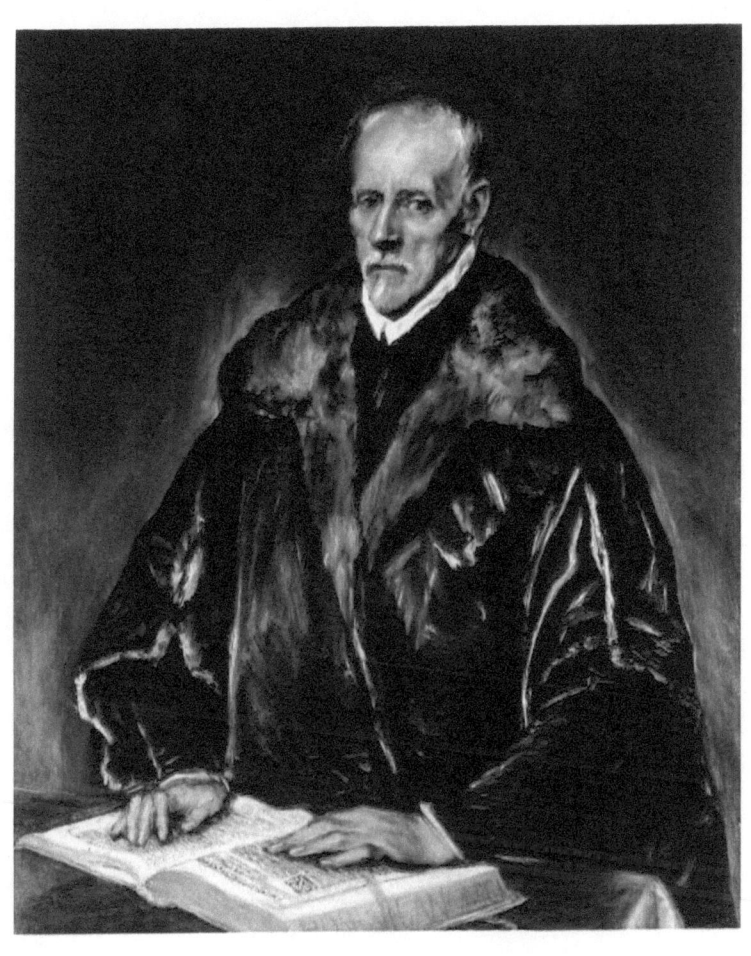

A Prelate, 1600s, Oil on canvas, 107 x 90 cm

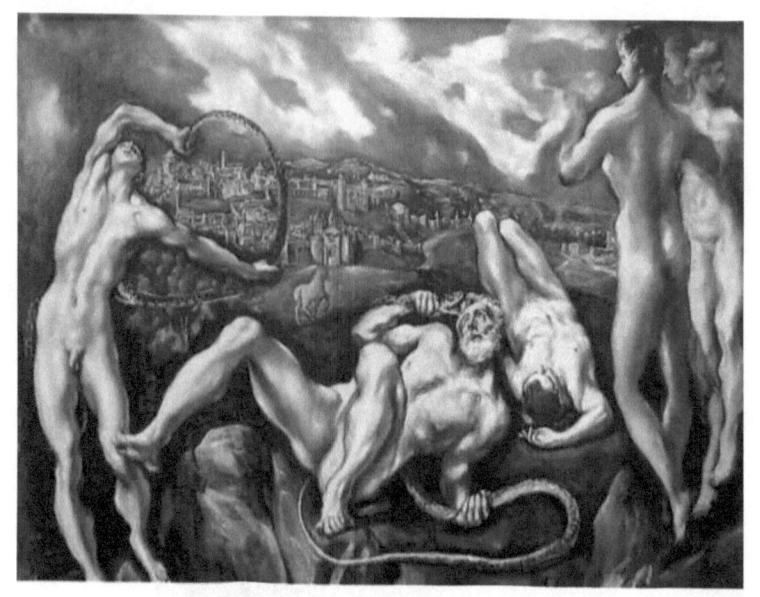

Laocoon, 1610, oil on canvas

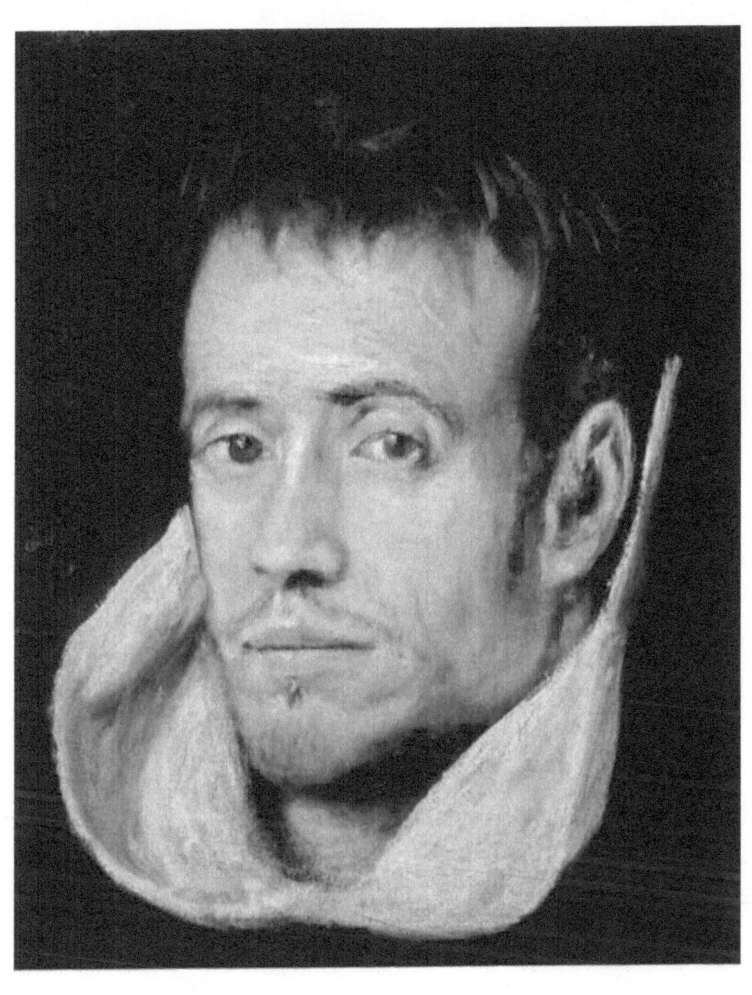

Portrait of a monk, 1610, oil on canvas

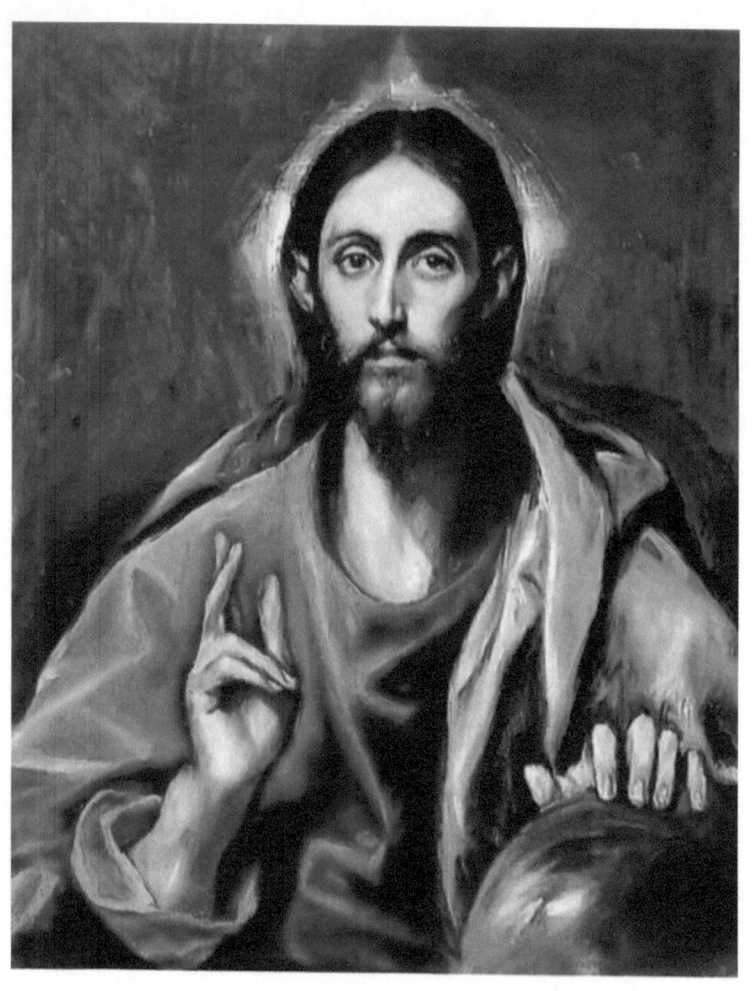

Savior, 1612, oil on canvas

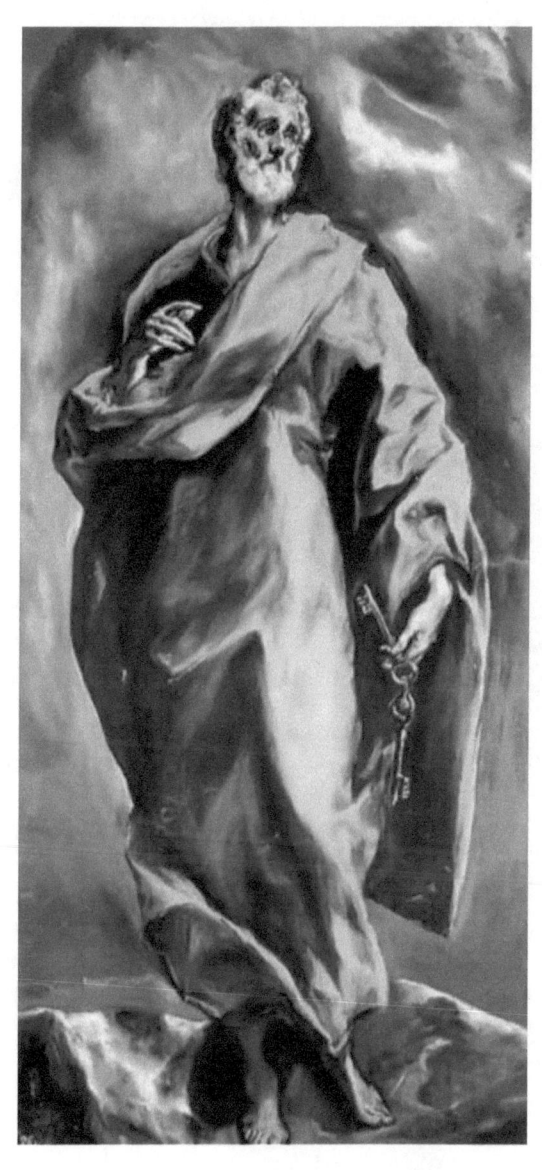

St. Peter, 1613, oil on canvas

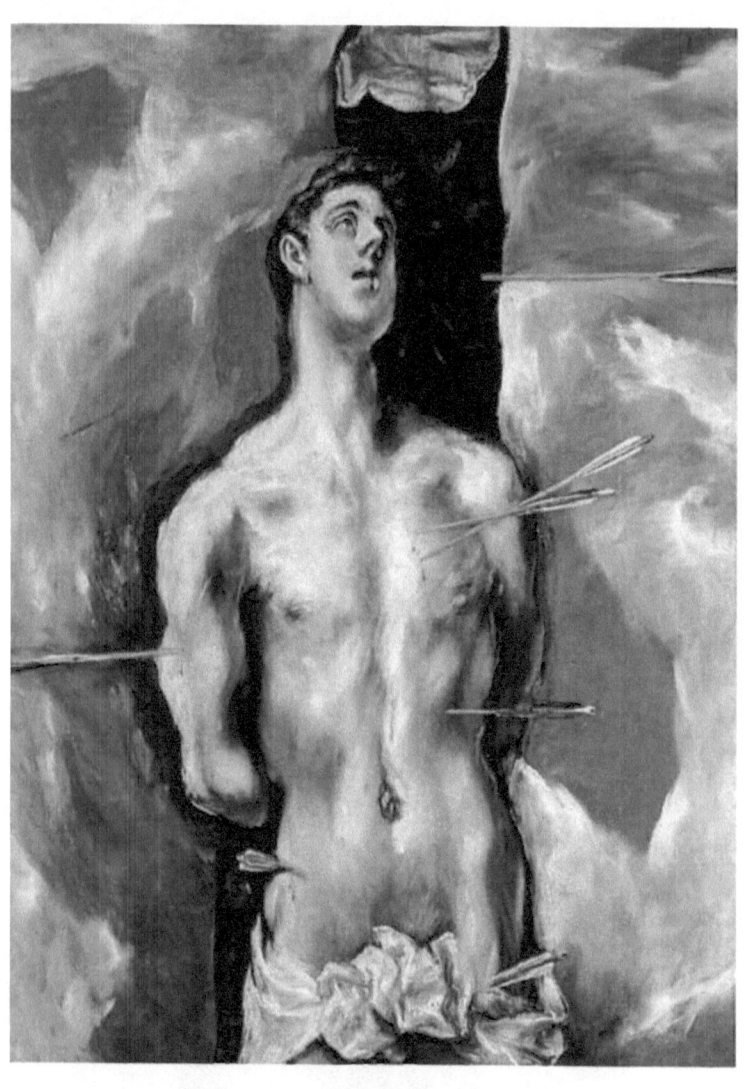

St. Sebastian, 1613, oil on canvas

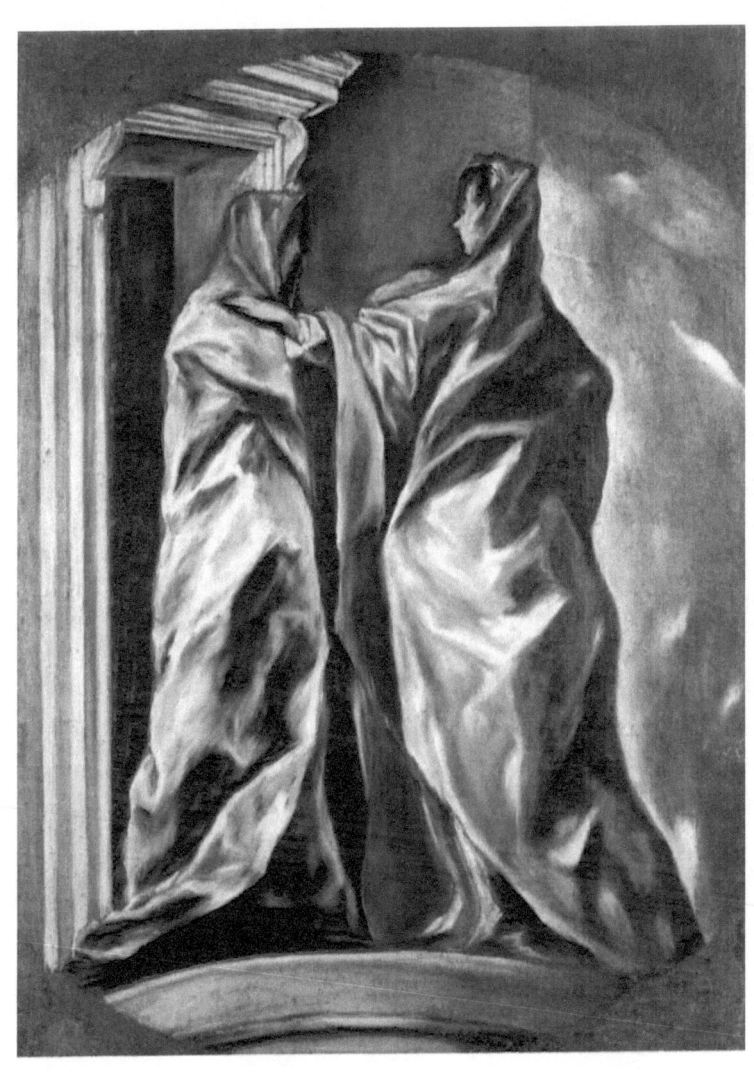

The Visitation, 1610-13, Oil on canvas, 96 x 72,4 cm

The Visitation was made for the Oballe Chapel in the Church of San Vicente in Toledo. It was intended to be framed and attached to the ceiling above The Virgin of the Immaculate Conception of the high altar. The intended location explains the dramatic sotto-in-su perspective of the scene, the curved rendering of the floor, and the absence of a horizon line. It does seem that the painting was originally within a circle, and that the canvas has been cut at the left and right.

The scene shows the meeting of Mary, on the right, pregnant with Jesus, and her cousin Elizabeth, who was in her sixth month awaiting the child who would become St John the Baptist. The meeting took place at the entrance to the house of Zachariah, the husband of Elizabeth. El Greco shows a classicising doorway with a heavy cornice and consoles on the left.

Like other works for the Oballe Chapel, The Visitation is painted with great force and dynamism.

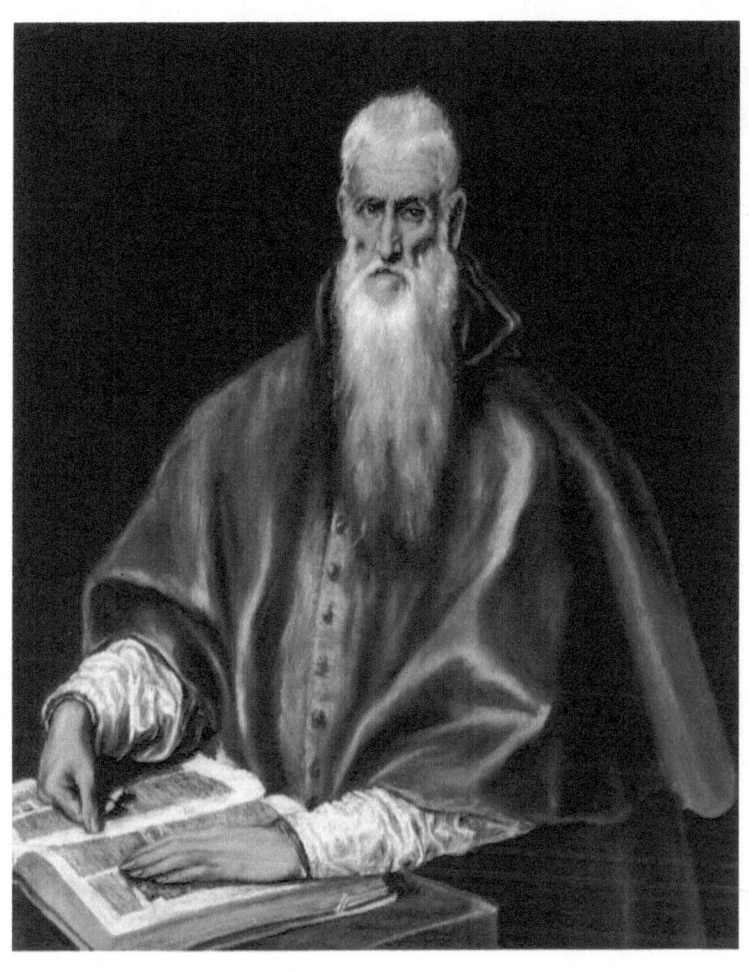

St Jerome as a Scholar, 1600-14, Oil on canvas, 108 x 89 cm

Endowed with an unsurpassed classical education, Jerome (c. 342-420) became an outstanding biblical scholar as well as the translator of the Bible into Latin (the Vulgate). During the Renaissance, paintings showing him either in his study or performing acts of penance in the wilderness adorned the walls of the homes of many humanists and scholars. El Greco painted both types. In this painting El Greco represented the scholar-cardinal standing behind his desk, marking his place with his thumb as he looks up, interrupted by an unexpected visitor. Five versions from El Greco's workshop and four copies are known, the two finest of which are in the Frick Collection, New York and the Metropolitan Museum.

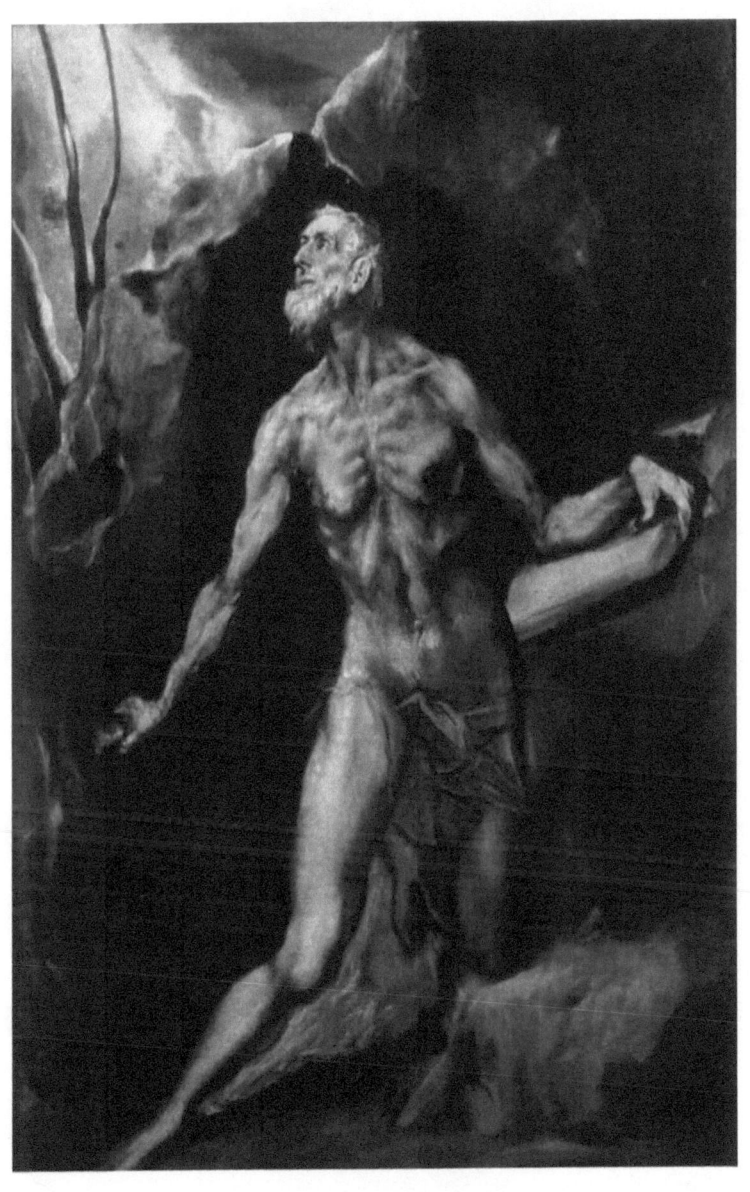

Saint Jerome Penitent, 1610-14, Oil on canvas, 166 x 110 cm

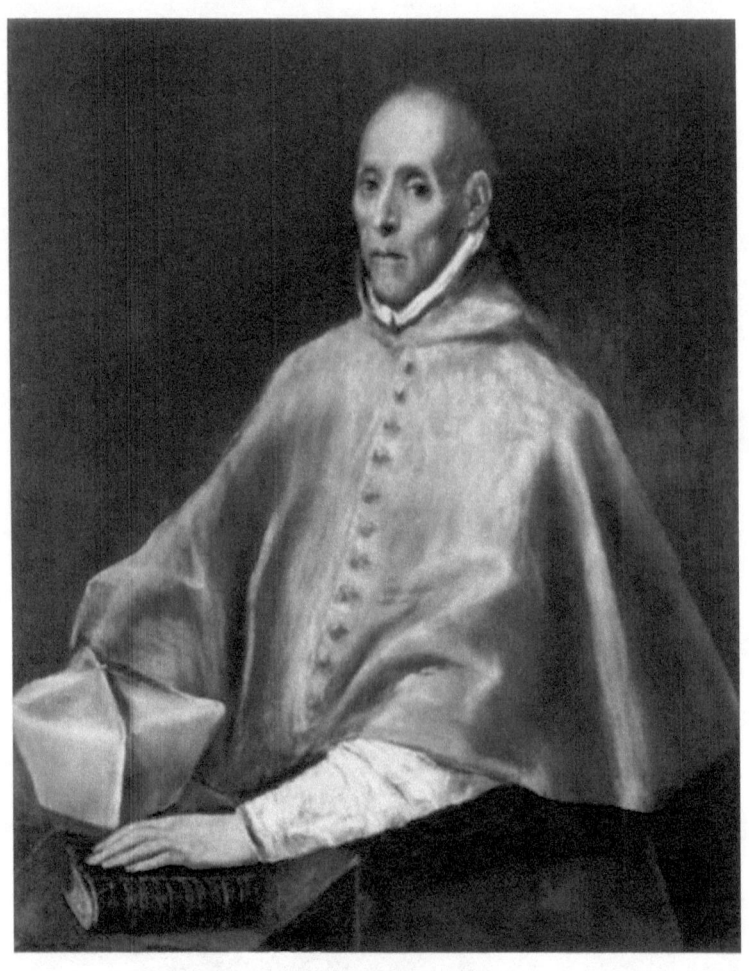

Portrait of Cardinal Tavera, 1608-14, Oil on canvas, 103
x 83 cm

This portrait is an example of El Greco's late work. Juan Pardo de Tavera (1472-1545) held both important ecclesiastical and political offices under Charles V, being active among other things as Grand Inquisitor and government chief of Castile. He founded in 1541 the Hospital de San Juan Bautista. By the time of his portrayal, however, he had long been deceased, the portrait was commissioned by Pedro Salazar de Mendoza, an important figure in Toledo's religious life, and the administrator of the Hospital de San Juan Bautista. The painting is signed at the bottom right.

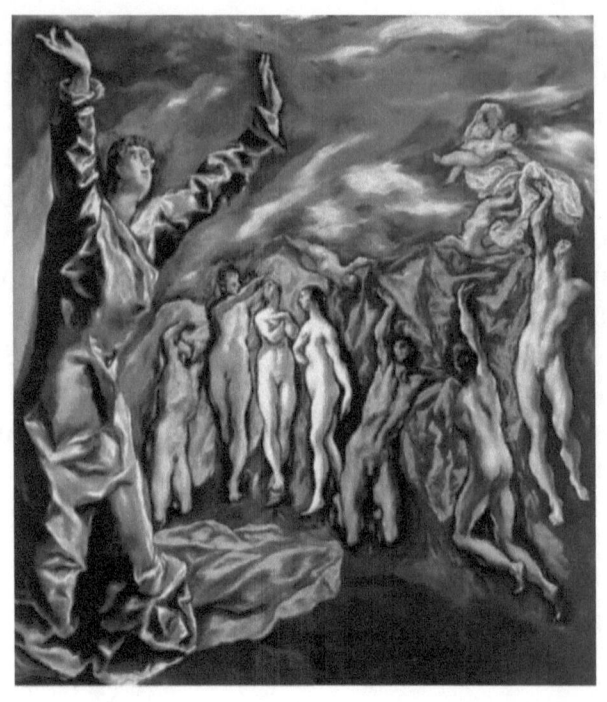

The vision of St. John (Apocalypse), 1614, oil on canvas